1974

k may be

THE REFERENCE SHELF   VOLUME 46 NUMBER 1

THE NATIONS
OF THE
INDIAN SUBCONTINENT

EDITED BY
IRWIN ISENBERG

Asia Bureau
United Nations Development Program

THE H. W. WILSON COMPANY
NEW YORK   1974

THE REFERENCE SHELF

The books in this series contain reprints of articles, excerpts from books, and addresses on current issues and social trends in the United States and other countries. There are six separately bound numbers in each volume, all of which are generally published in the same calendar year. One number is a collection of recent speeches; each of the others is devoted to a single subject and gives background information and discussion from various points of view, concluding with a comprehensive bibliography. Books in the series may be purchased individually or on subscription.

Copyright © 1974
By The H. W. Wilson Company
PRINTED IN THE UNITED STATES OF AMERICA

Library of Congress Cataloging in Publication Data

Isenberg, Irwin, comp.
    The nations of the Indian subcontinent.

    (The Reference shelf, v. 46, no. 1)
    Bibliography: p.
    1. South Asia. I. Title. II. Series.
DS335.I8   915.4   74-1346
ISBN 0-8242-0521-9

PREFACE

The countries of India, Bangladesh, Pakistan, and Sri Lanka (formerly known as Ceylon) contain more than 700 million people—nearly 20 percent of the globe's population. That alone makes this area of the world important.

Although each of these four south Asian countries has its distinctive characteristics, they have much in common. Each is poor, overpopulated, and largely agricultural. Each has a long and rich cultural background. Most of the people live in small villages and have little contact with the cities. Unemployment and illiteracy are high; per capita income and productivity are low. Malnutrition is common and adequate social services uncommon. Each of the four countries is plagued by a host of social and economic problems which defy quick solution, threaten stability, and hinder progress.

The Western countries usually give primary attention to India because of its size in area and population and the consequent magnitude of its problems, such as recurrent droughts and famines and the depths of its poverty, and because of its well-known and much respected leaders—Gandhi, Jawaharlal Nehru, and the current prime minister, Indira Gandhi. In addition, the West has closely followed India's fortunes because of India's commitment to democratic political forms. Moreover, in the cold-war context, India was considered a leader of the nonaligned or neutral nations.

Since 1971, however, the West has also been much concerned with Bangladesh, formerly East Pakistan. Bangladesh became independent after a bitter guerrilla war against Pakistan in 1971 and a two-week battle between India and Pakistan in December 1971. Since then, headlines have brought the world's attention to bear upon the new nation's

3

attempts to survive under the most difficult conditions.
These efforts have been aided by a massive and relatively
successful global relief operation to prevent starvation and
tackle the formidable challenges of rehabilitation and reconstruction.

Pakistan is of special interest because it was allied mili-
tarily to the United States in the 1950s and 1960s and was
regarded as an anti-Communist outpost in Asia. Though
still in force, this alliance has become less crucial in recent
years as a result of the improvement in relations between
the United States and the Communist countries of China
and the Soviet Union. Pakistan's primary foreign policy
concern, apart from Bangladesh, has been India and the
still unresolved dispute over the Himalayan state of Kashmir,
which is governed by India though claimed by Pakistan.
(During the 1971 India-Pakistan war over Bangladesh,
skirmishes also were fought in Kashmir.) As India has
moved somewhat closer to the Soviet Union in recent years,
Pakistan has improved its relations with China.

Sri Lanka, because of its relatively small population and
remoteness from major international issues, is little written
about or discussed in the West. But, as an offshore island of
the great subcontinental land mass, it is closely involved in
issues concerning India and Pakistan and is thus of importance in regional issues.

While no single book can encompass India, Bangladesh,
Pakistan, and Sri Lanka adequately, this volume examines
the area's major political, economic, and social issues. The
first section deals with the historical perspective, political
background, and economic setting in general terms. Current
questions should be considered in the context of these broad
areas.

The second section briefly sketches the social system as
exposed through caste differences in India, the seclusion of
women in Pakistan, and the general attitudes of varied
groups. It is important to appreciate the values and beliefs
of the people because they have had a powerful influence in

the past and continue to be a major factor in subcontinental life. However, it should be stressed that in many respects the social systems of traditional societies are far more complex than those known in the West.

The third section concentrates on the economy of India, a subject which itself could easily fill a large volume. As will be seen from the selection of articles, there are grounds to be both pessimistic and reasonably optimistic for the future. Although there has been considerable and often astonishing progress in some fields, many of the most basic problems have become more serious as a consequence of population growth, which results in a net increase of some 13 million people annually.

The last section reviews some of the pertinent political and economic questions in Bangladesh, Pakistan, and Sri Lanka. As in India, these issues often divide themselves into two categories: those dealing with the immediate problems and those concerning long-term attempts to stimulate national progress.

The editor wishes to thank the publishers and authors who have granted permission to reprint the selections in this compilation. The editor also wishes to thank Barbara Webb for her generous assistance.

IRWIN ISENBERG

January 1974

CONTENTS

PREFACE 3

MAP: The Nations of the Indian Subcontinent 10

I. A SUBCONTINENTAL VIEW

Editor's Introduction 11

Wayne A. Wilcox. India and Pakistan: The Background 12

W. Norman Brown. The Indian Subcontinent Today .. 26

Irwin Isenberg. The Subcontinent: A Different World 46

II. THE PEOPLE: HOW THEY LIVE

Editor's Introduction 59

Irwin Isenberg. The Caste System 60

Bernard Weinraub. Pakistan's P.O.W. Wives ....
.... New York Times 72

Bernard D. Nossiter. Indifferent India ....
.... New Republic 75

India's Endless Troubles ... U.S. News & World Report 83

Bernard Weinraub. Urban Squalor ....
.... New York Times 93

For India: The Key to Development ....
.... Development Forum 96

III. THE INDIAN ECONOMY

Editor's Introduction 101

Robert R. R. Brooks. Can India Make It? ....
.... Saturday Review 102

Phillips Talbot. The Economic Struggle 113

Richard Critchfield. Punjab, Bengal and the Green
    Revolution .... Nation 126

William D. Hartley. Parched Land ....
.... Wall Street Journal 136

Kasturi Rangan. India's Planning Goes Awry ....
.... New York Times 143

IV. BANGLADESH, PAKISTAN, AND SRI LANKA

Editor's Introduction 147

Bangladesh: The Fight for Survival ...... Newsweek 148

Lewis M. Simons. On First Anniversary, Bangladesh's
    Future Still a Question Mark .... Washington Post 154

Ayub Khan's "Basic Democracy" 163

Khurshid Hyder. Pakistan Under Bhutto ....
.... Current History 169

Elizabeth Gilliland. Ceylon: The Bitter Harvest ......
.... Nation 184

BIBLIOGRAPHY 189

THE NATIONS OF THE INDIAN SUBCONTINENT

From "India and Pakistan." In *Great Decisions 1967*. Foreign Policy Association. 345 E. 46th St. New York, N.Y. 10017. '67. p 13. Adapted with permission.

I. A SUBCONTINENTAL VIEW

EDITOR'S INTRODUCTION

Since the end of World War II in 1945, the subcontinent frequently has been in turmoil. In 1947, the British gave up their colony of India, which then divided into two countries: a predominantly Hindu India and a predominantly Muslim Pakistan. The new nation of Pakistan was composed of two wings—East and West Pakistan—separated by one thousand miles of Indian territory. Widespread and bloody rioting accompanied this partition as Hindus and Muslims migrated by the millions. In 1971, East Pakistan successfully revolted against West Pakistan and became the independent country of Bangladesh.

India and Pakistan have gone to war three times since the partition. They fought in 1947 over the disputed territory of Kashmir, again in 1965, and in 1971 as India went to the aid of Bangladesh. In several other instances, both nations mobilized their troops but war was averted. In 1962 India also fought a brief war against China in the remote northeastern regions bordering the two countries. Only Sri Lanka (formerly Ceylon) has been immune from conflict with an external power.

All four countries in this region have been buffeted by serious internal strife on the political, economic, labor, and social fronts. India has had to cope with severe labor and social problems which often have resulted in violence. In addition, the state governments of India's federal system have frequently been in contention with the central authority.

Pakistan has been plagued by recurrent political instability, which finally resulted in the birth of Bangladesh. The new nation of Bangladesh is itself trying to cope with overwhelming economic and social problems. Sri Lanka too has had its share of political and economic headaches.

This section outlines some of these issues so that current questions can be better understood. The first article recalls the events and conditions which led to the 1947 partition and analyzes the consequences of the split in political and economic terms. This article explains why Socialist thought and practice took root in India to a greater extent than in Pakistan, where capitalist enterprise dominated the economy.

The second selection, taken from a book by W. Norman Brown, one of the leading authorities on South Asia, presents a broad view of India, Pakistan, and Bangladesh today. This article concentrates on the geographic and climatic features and the basic economic realities which dominate life on the subcontinent.

The third article discusses the similarities and the differences among the four countries concerned. In particular, it offers a description of village life. The extract also speaks of urban life and then describes some of the rich and varied cultural features of the subcontinent.

Together, these three selections present a general view of the subcontinent and serve as an introduction to the specific topics reviewed in subsequent sections.

INDIA AND PAKISTAN: THE BACKGROUND [1]

In August 1947, the British abandoned their prized imperial citadel in the Indian subcontinent and, in the midst of communal strife that claimed some 600,000 lives and created 10 million refugees, turned power over to the two new governments of India and Pakistan. The political fortunes of the two new nations have been quite different, but both have contended with the awesome burdens of poverty, il-

[1] From *India and Pakistan*, pamphlet by Wayne A. Wilcox, professor of government, Columbia University. (Headline Series no 185) Foreign Policy Association. '67. p 3-18. Reprinted by permission from Headline Series no 185. Copyright 1967 by the Foreign Policy Association, Inc. 345 E. 46th St. New York 10017.

literacy, national insecurity and explosive population growth. Pakistan lost its great leader, Mohammed Ali Jinnah, after little more than a year of independence, and India's Mahatma M. K. Gandhi was assassinated a few months after the end of British rule. Younger leaders, Jawaharlal Nehru in India and Liaquat Ali Khan in Pakistan, then took charge and set their nations unsteadily on a course toward parliamentary government. Liaquat Ali Khan was assassinated in 1951, however, and Pakistan's cabinets grew progressively more unstable until a military coup d'état in October 1958 installed General Mohammed Ayub Khan as president. [Pakistan is now ruled by President Z. A. Bhutto. —Ed.] Nehru continued to lead India until his death in 1964. Lal Bahadur Shastri replaced Nehru as prime minister, but died two years later in Tashkent, USSR, and was succeeded by Mrs. Indira Gandhi, Jawaharlal Nehru's only child and a prominent Congress party official. . . .

India and Pakistan, though neighbors, inherited very dissimilar social and political soils; the distribution of the British imperial legacy was even more diverse.

In the period of British rule almost all of India's economic development was concentrated in the great cities of Calcutta, Bombay and Madras. From these centers the transportation network spread out. Bombay's growing textile industry was well served by a fertile cotton-growing plain around it; Calcutta's heavy industry had the sinews of Bihar's coal and eastern India's iron ore. The British port cities attracted vigorous and ambitious sons of the soil, and the new British colleges and universities soon . . . [produced] a class of persons, Indian in blood and color, but English in taste, in opinions, in morals and in intellect.

The port cities of British India opened the subcontinent to European trade and ideas, which stimulated the rise and development of the nationalist movement. By the end of the nineteenth century India's urban elites were considering a future of freedom within the British Empire and were experiencing the first stages of the development of a modern economy and state. Two decades later the nationalist movement gained new impetus in the wake of changes wrought by the Russo-Japanese War, World War I and the Bolshevik revolution in Russia. . . .

It was Gandhi who turned Indian nationalism from an urban Hindu and Muslim elite movement, limited in its impact to no more than 10 percent of the population, into a mass movement that reached into smaller towns and captured the popular imagination. But it was also Gandhi who unwittingly magnified the differences between Indian Hindus and Indian Muslims with his emphasis on mass participation, majority rule and Indian (Hindu) tradition.

Muslims became apprehensive that majority rule and Hindu revivalism would undermine their faith and dim their political future. After the electoral disasters of 1937, in which Muslim candidates were badly defeated and the Congress was triumphant in provincial elections, the Muslim League became the symbol of and vehicle for Muslim demands. Mohammed Ali Jinnah, the league's leader, who was once called the ambassador of Hindu-Muslim unity, was not a religious fanatic. But more than any other Muslim man of affairs, he was an able organizer and fund raiser, a tenacious advocate and a man whom the Indian Muslims came to trust fully as they became more fearful of the Hindu majority.

Pakistan's Inheritance

Because communal distrust rose as Indian nationalism grew, nationalists divided into two streams. After World War II had exhausted the British, the streams rose in a flood to produce Muslim Pakistan as well as independent India. Pakistan, divided into two wings on either side of the subcontinent, found one thousand miles of Indian territory separating the halves of the country. In the west, Pakistan embraced the irrigated desert of the Indus Valley, the largest irrigated area on the earth's surface. In the east, Pakistan was a marshy delta subject to annual floods and heavy monsoon rains. West Pakistan produced wheat, sugar cane and cotton, while East Pakistan grew jute and rice. Lahore, the largest city of the new country in 1947 . . . had never been more than the capital city of a rural Indian province. Karachi, the first federal capital . . . was then a sun-baked provincial town on the Arabian sea. Dacca, the capital of East Pakistan, was a district town languishing in the tall shadow of its close neighbor, Calcutta, where almost all of the industrial plant of Bengal was centered.

The total electrical generating capacity of Pakistan in 1947 was only a little over 75,000 Kw, of which East Pakistan's share was a scant 15,600 Kw. Three times the size of Italy, Pakistan had but 75 bank branches for its 80 million people. It inherited only 14 of the nearly 400 cotton textile mills of British India, and none of the jute mills, despite the fact that East Pakistan grew about 75 percent of all the jute of the subcontinent. Pakistan's army, largely composed of infantry units, was unsupported by even one ordnance plant; its civilian bureaucracy numbered a mere eighty-two former members of the elite Indian Civil Service (ICS). The soil of Pakistan did not appear capable of supporting the seed of a Muslim nation, let alone the weak plant of a new government at Karachi in 1947.

India's Inheritance

The British partition award allotted 82.5 percent of all British Indian resources to independent India; all fixed assets, such as railways, museums, schools, post offices and communication facilities, were to remain in the territory in which they were located. This settlement and the nature of the division of territory gave India almost all of the capital plant and social resources of British India. The major cost of partition to India was in agricultural lands: 31 million acres of irrigated land in the Punjab fell to Pakistan and exacerbated India's wheat shortages; also important was the loss of 40 percent of the raw cotton and 75 percent of the raw jute production. . . .

India inherited, for good or ill, almost all that was the British empire in India—its bureaucrats and its buildings, its soldiers and its shops, its poets and its ports. India's creation as a state was accompanied by the secession of most of its Muslims, but India thereafter found itself a more homogeneous political community. Gandhi, the father of the country, and Nehru, its Jefferson, symbolized the meeting of the old and new. . . .

Tests of Survival

The first few years in the life of a new state are critical. If leaders can maintain unity and if the weight of decision-making responsibility does not overwhelm them, there is a good chance that orderly politics will become a habit, part of a national way of doing things. Popular confidence breeds political courage and strong leadership. If peace can be maintained, a garrison state need not be erected to protect a tenuous national personality. Perhaps even more important, the choices made in the first years create an environment that limits the range of future choices. During the first years of independence, India and Pakistan faced five general problems that called for fundamental action: (1) governmental inexperience in democratic nation-building; (2) mass poverty and illiteracy; (3) tense relationships between administrators and politicians; (4) potential federal disunity in a linguistically plural continent; and (5) national insecurity and a war for Kashmir.

Political Inexperience and Popular Democracy

While it is true that the British progressively created new opportunities for Indian political participation during their last three decades of rule, the segment of the population that was allowed to vote in various kinds of elections never exceeded 15 percent of the adult population. Until the 1935 Government of India Act opened many new provincial legislatures, there were, in fact, very few parliamentary seats for politicians. World War II cut short the widespread schooling in democratic responsibility that began in the provincial elections of 1937; independence came abruptly in 1947 in a period characterized by civil violence and political uncertainty. The nationalist movement trained politicians in the tactics and techniques of agitation and resistance, but the growth of opportunities to learn "the ethic of responsibility" in government was much less ample. It is easier to organize people *not* to pay land taxes than it is to convince them to pay higher taxes for the common good.

The nationalist slogans promised much—land reform and economic growth, prosperity, dignity in the world, the end to foreign law, culture and values. Future Pakistanis were promised an Islamic state, whatever that was, while future Indians were promised social welfare, an end to indignity and a secular state, whatever that was. And while Mohammed Ali Jinnah called the Muslims to "faith, unity and discipline," and Nehru warned that Indians would "have to labor and to work, and work hard, to give reality" to their dreams, thousands of ordinary party workers were spreading the notion that once the British ceased stealing the wealth of Hindustan, there would automatically be more for everyone.

Neither the nationalist leaders nor their followers were quite prepared for the hard choices, the austerity and the competition of independence. The Indian and Pakistani governments found it necessary to keep much of the inherited legislation dealing with civil disorder . . . because they did not know how else to control it. In the first three years of independence, the Indian government doubled the number of police in a period of unprecedented civil and economic strife. In 1948 and 1949 there were almost 2,200 strikes that led to the loss of 14.5 million man-days. Gandhi was assassinated by a right-wing Hindu fanatic. Thousands of refugees clogged the main cities of India demanding that "their" government do something about their plight. Communists in Telengana, in Hyderabad state, were directing a violent insurgency.

Pakistan was slightly more free of industrial strife, largely because it had so little industry, but the demand of refugees for effective help and the complete breakdown of normal government services in the aftermath of partition posed even greater burdens on a much weaker government. Jinnah's death removed the great arbiter and dramatic figure from the seat of power, and Liaquat Ali Khan's strengths were organizational, not charismatic. The survival of Pakistan can be credited to the work of the civil service and the army, and to the desperation of the refugees who understood that the promised land would be of their making or it would not be at all.

Yet in neither India nor Pakistan was there immediate effective support for political leadership as an alternative to administrative dominance in government. Jawaharlal Nehru and Sardar Vallabhai Patel struggled for control of the Indian government until the latter's ill-health and death removed him from active contention. Politicians struggled against one another in Pakistan until they were nearly all discredited. The hard tasks of winning support from a public that had never participated in democratic politics, and that had unrealistically high expectations of what government could do, proved a trying task. Only the most dedicated democrats could summon up the courage to risk an election in Pakistan, and many of them and their more numerous cousins in India were thrown out by an electorate whose judgment was as untried as that of the candidates.

In India the Congress party protected and elected many of its loyal supporters. With money, hard work, party loyalty and Congress support, most candidates could win at least one election in almost any constituency in India. So long as the Congress was strong and the voters loyal to it, politicians could afford to trust their fate to a democratic system in which their particular skills were valued and in which they were reasonably secure. For this reason more than for any other, a democratic Indian political system was erected and strengthened in the first years of independence.

In Pakistan, the Muslim League party that had emerged victorious in the eleventh hour of an uncertain nationalist struggle was a curious organization. Its major leaders had their roots in Bombay and the United Provinces in India; yet their new national "home" was the Punjab, Sind, North-West Frontier Province and Bengal, where historically they had little support. The national political elite of Pakistan, therefore, found themselves with new constituencies, often dominated by hostile provincial leaders who could capitalize on local loyalties directed against "outsiders." Of the new countries in the world, Pakistan was unique in having a nationalist elite that lacked substantive and widespread support in the territory that became the state.

The struggle for political leadership in the country took place less on personal or ideological grounds than on the basis of provincial rivalries and local loyalties. Liaquat Ali Khan was the last of the refugee leaders. After his assassination the future of political life in the country was in the hands of the civil service and the army, whose officers did not need to fear elections; and provincial leaders who, strong in their own locality, sought to capture the central government by creating provincial coalitions. Since there was no political security in elections and no democracy without them, the national leaders delayed the writing of a constitution, postponed elections and temporized on establishing popular representative institutions by emphasizing, instead, ideology. In contrast to India, Pakistan had an inexperienced and weak nationalist party and a divided, parochial electorate, neither of which could either maintain the inherited semidemocratic structure of the last days of British rule or reduce the decisive risks of democratic politics.

Poverty and Illiteracy

It came as an unpleasant shock to leaders in India and Pakistan to learn that their economic and social conditions were even worse than they had themselves pictured them in nationalist pamphlets. Literacy, loosely defined, was no more than 17 percent and was scattered among peoples reading many more than a dozen languages. The annual per capita income was about $53 (roughly three times that in purchasing power). World War II had led to great inflation, with the general price index rising from 100 in 1939 to 310.4 in August 1947, the month of partition and independence. Eight million new Indians and almost two million new Pakistanis were being added to the population every year. Refugees flooded into cities of the new states, creating major public health problems and straining already insufficient water, sewage, electricity, schooling and transportation facilities. And in the 600,000 villages of the subcontinent there were many who did not yet know they were free citizens of an independent country, and who knew even less about the impact of their individual acts on the success or failure of those new governments.

Jawaharlal Nehru was a political economist by interest if not training. Socialism and developmental economics fascinated him, and, on the eve of independence, he believed that only purposive, directed planning could possibly save India from the "low-level equilibrium trap" in which it was caught. Because the people were poor and had no savings, there was little capital to invest. Nehru's views on Socialist (or, perhaps more accurately, public welfare) planning triggered a noisy debate, for India's business leaders believed that the free market offered the best chances for Indian development as well as for their own prosperity. This rivalry of viewpoint was converted into the "private sector-public sector" competition that has characterized the Indian economic dialogue. . . .

Pakistan's political leadership was notably lacking in economists. Jinnah's successor as governor general of Pakistan, Ghulam Mohammed, had served the famous Tata firm as a director. He believed that men of genius should serve business, not government, but he was himself trained as a civil servant. The Aga Khan called upon his followers in Bombay to move to Pakistan to conduct business, but many cautiously waited to see if the new state would survive. Most of the bankers and entrepreneurs who had been in Pakistan before independence were Hindu, and they felt understandably uncomfortable about the place of Hindu private enterprise in an Islamic state.

As a result of the notable absence of economic talent in the cabinet (or, for that matter, in the country at large) and policy predilections, the government of Pakistan followed an almost complete laissez-faire policy. It invited entrepreneurs to come to Pakistan to establish businesses and offered tariff protection for the infant enterprises. Businesses were guaranteed against nationalization, and little mention of socialism and social welfare policies was found in the public rhetoric of Pakistan's leaders. As a result, capitalist enterprise became Pakistan's principal engine of economic growth. . . .

Thus India and Pakistan followed different policies toward economic and social growth, India venturing further toward state participation in social and economic change.

Administration, the Army and Politicians

The British system of government in India was autocratic. It was based upon police forces backed by a highly trained professional army. Its agents were the few British who dominated the higher posts in the civil service, the courts and commercial enterprises. When India and Pakistan became independent, they inherited a system of government based on bureaucratic and military supremacy, and they also inherited bureaucrats and soldiers trained in that tradition.

Political leadership, therefore, found itself with twin tasks: subordinating the praetorian system of administrative autocracy without destroying its efficiency and ensuring that the military services were kept out of politics and directed primarily at external foes. These were difficult tasks because attempts at political control over administrators were labeled "interference" dangerous to morale and efficiency.

Treating soldiers as servants and not masters was equally difficult, especially since they had guns and politicians did not.

In Pakistan, the weak state was held together by a loyal and effective civil service supported by an efficient and loyal army. They served Pakistan even during its tense moments of political instability, but they viewed interference with their prerogatives as unwarranted. "Ministers come and go," they would argue, "but civil servants must stay to clean up the mess and ensure that there will be a future." Since the civil service had such a relatively high level of competence, and since Pakistan was such a tenuous political community, its political leaders did not attempt to reduce administrative autonomy; in fact, they encouraged civil servants to direct various ministries.

The army was also viewed without hostility by political leadership. Its officers and men had bravely brought refugees across the Punjab into Pakistan, they had sealed off a tribal rebellion along the North-West Frontier Province and they had fought well and loyally in Kashmir against a stronger foe. The nation had reason to value its troops as Indo-Pakistan relations deteriorated in the years after partition and Pakistan's security was threatened.

Pakistan's political leaders were fighting for the survival of the state, and every element of strength had to be bolstered. Because of their unique positions, both the civil service and the army had top-priority claims on national resources in the first years of independence, and both used their claims well.

India's political leaders were more confident and their nation more secure. Dedicated to political supremacy, they meant to substitute cabinet authority for secretaries' administrative authority throughout the state. Nehru and his colleagues, being suspicious of the army, took every opportunity to isolate it in domestic politics. Both the Home (civil intelligence and police) and Defense ministries were managed by Nehru's personal lieutenants in the Congress party, and when he showed preference among civil servants for higher civil-service posts, his decisions carried crucial weight. Moreover, he created and then led a "supercabinet," the Planning Commission, which had extensive planning and reviewing powers. It was an alternative bureaucracy intended to monitor and direct operating ministries of the government and to keep the prime minister informed about the responsiveness of the traditional bureaucracy to political leadership.

Unity and Disunity in a Plural Society

The Congress party, as early as 1920, organized itself into linguistic units. The Indian Constitution now recognizes sixteen official languages. Pakistan, on the other hand, is attempting to work out a three-language formula—Bengali, Urdu and English—although there is opposition from those who speak Punjabi, Pushtu, Sindhi, Baluchi and Gujarati.

Both Jawaharlal Nehru and Mohammed Ali Jinnah wanted their countries to have one language as a vehicle for common national expression. Nehru probably favored English, which he viewed both as an international and a technical language and which Indians had begun to learn in large numbers, but he understood that many Indians would insist upon an indigenous language. (Hindi, spoken by most of the inhabitants of the Ganges valley of northern India is the largest single language bloc of the many major Indian languages.) Jinnah and most of his associates spoke English but favored Urdu, which was the historic language of the Moghuls as well as a flexible and beautiful language akin to Hindi, but written in the Arabic-Persian script.

Yet no single language offered a politically acceptable choice in either country. Hindi was used by no more than 40 percent of the Indian population. Many of the other languages of the subcontinent are more sophisticated literary languages, and all hold special meaning to those who speak them. In Pakistan, English and Urdu were acceptable only to the dominant urban and rural elites and both seemed to eliminate Bengali-speakers from the national dialogue. In 1952 there were language riots in both Pakistan and India, and the fast unto death of a political leader in the Telugu-speaking region of Madras, later called Andhra Pradesh, led to the creation of that state.

Widespread violence and the absence of an acceptable alternative has forced both governments to temporize on the language issue. The "three language formula" (allowing the use of the local language in strictly local business, Urdu or Hindi in national business and English for certain categories of transstate and national business) has been employed as a pragmatic solution.

Provincial sentiment organized around deep loyalties to language and regional culture can represent a threat to national unity. Around such sentiments have grown other interests—political, educational and economic—that trade on provincial differences. For the foreseeable future, therefore, India and Pakistan will be linguistically heterogeneous states and the central governments of both will face important tasks of federal coordination.

National Insecurity and the Kashmir War

No sooner had the British left India than a war broke out over Kashmir, the large, lovely, princely state in the western Himalayas. Under the British partition plan, princely states were to have the option of joining either India or Pakistan, depending upon their location and other factors. Kashmir is contiguous to Pakistan but also connected to India. Its people are predominantly Muslim, but the maharaja, army and aristocracy were Hindu. In late 1947, when communal rioting and refugee exchanges were convulsing all of Northern India and West Pakistan, a Muslim rebellion broke out in Poonch, a district in western Jammu. Aimed at forcing the maharaja out of power and joining Kashmir to Pakistan, the rebellion was harshly suppressed by the local government but not before large numbers of tribesmen from the North-West Frontier of Pakistan and Afghanistan invaded Kashmir. The maharaja thereupon acceded to India and called for Indian troops to be flown into Kashmir for defense. As Indian troops began to win the undeclared war and to push even more refugees toward Pakistan's frontiers, the British general (on loan to command the new army) sent regular Pakistani troops into battle to stabilize the front. The Indian and Pakistani governments agreed to a United Nations-arranged cease-fire agreement to start on January 1, 1949, and the dispute has remained rancorous since that time.

The Indian cabinet, through a formal statement by Governor General Lord Mountbatten, accepted the accession of the ruler of Kashmir "subject to a reference to the people." Since the UN armistice was viewed as preliminary to an international settlement, many Pakistanis believed that a "plebiscite" would be held as agreed by both parties in 1949 and Kashmir would join Pakistan. India complained that Pakistan would not pull its troops out of the portion of Kashmiri territory they occupied before the "reference to the people" and made clear that it considered the legislative assembly elections held in the state as its fulfillment of the pledge. In any case, New Delhi insisted that Kashmir was legally Indian.

The outcome of the first Kashmiri war, the nature of the partition disputes and the superiority of India on the field of battle left Pakistan frustrated, embittered and insecure. In the years between 1949 and 1963, India mobilized along Pakistan's frontiers three times. After armed clashes at the Rann of Cutch in September 1965, war broke out between Pakistan and India, first in Kashmir and then all along the West Pakistan-Indian frontier.

The national insecurity of Pakistan permeated all segments of the society. It led to the building of a large military establishment, a public commitment to force India to give the Kashmiris a "choice" and an unremitting hostility toward India. Indian leaders' sense of security and their near hegemony in the subcontinent permitted them to minimize the attention paid to military development. Its leaders felt they could afford peaceful development; Pakistan thought it could afford no less than a garrison state.

THE INDIAN SUBCONTINENT TODAY [2]

When the old "British Indian Empire" was partitioned and made into the two nations of India and Pakistan on August 15, 1947, enthusiasts in the two countries celebrated the event in somewhat the spirit of welcoming the arrival of the millennium. In India in 1947 it was thought by many who had been promoting the cause of nationalism that full self-rule (*purna swaraj*), in freeing the country from colonialism, would automatically and quickly lead to progressive release from economic exploitation and bring prosperity and resolution of the country's many problems—economic, social, and political. . . . There were, of course, many other Indians, like Jawaharlal Nehru, more sophisticated in outlook and more experienced in public affairs, who knew better. They realized that it would take a long, hard, uphill pull to achieve even a moderate degree of progress.

In Pakistan the prevailing public expectation about the attainment of national goals through independence was even less realistic than that in India. Partly the difference was due to the fact that the goals were in some important respects less in keeping with twentieth century political aims than India's goals. Pakistan had come into being because the Muslims in prepartition India wanted to live in and have as their own an Islamic state, governed by Muslims and operated for the benefit of Muslims and the fulfillment of Muslim religious ideals. The millennium for them was to be a Muslim one, with a predominantly Muslim population happily released from Hindu—or Christian—dominance. Living in an Islamic state, not only would they enjoy religious preferential treatment but all their economic, social, and politi-

[2] From *The United States and India, Pakistan, Bangladesh*, by W. Norman Brown, professor of South Asia studies, University of Pennsylvania. 3d ed. Harvard University Press. '72. p 1-18. Copyright © 1953, 1963, 1972 by the President and Fellows of Harvard College. Reprinted by permission of the publishers.

cal institutions would be informed with Islamic religious principles. The constitution subsequently framed stated at the beginning that the state was to be Islamic. Secularism did not enter into the thinking of the framers of the constitutions which were successively adopted and then abandoned. There were, to be sure, more sophisticated members of the nation, some of them with modern views, but they were generally muted and unheard. In the succeeding years the expectations of the strongly religiously motivated Pakistanis have been only partly fulfilled amid the nation's pressing, and often conflicting, needs and goals. At the same time the economic advance that was hoped for in 1947 has not been met, while the political situation has been unsettled and finally erupted in civil war in 1971, which in 1972 led to the creation of the new nation Bangladesh. . . .

The partition of the British Indian Empire had been made on the basis of assigning to Pakistan, as far as was feasible, predominantly Muslim parts of India that were contiguous. Application of this principle led to the creation of Pakistan as a nation of two parts separated from each other by a distance of 920 miles, with all the intervening territory belonging to India. The old prepartition India, a self-contained subcontinent, well isolated from the rest of the world by difficult land barriers and sea, had about 1,581,410 square miles of territory, less than four ninths the area of the United States. This was divided unequally between India and Pakistan in a ratio of not quite 3.4 to 1, with some regions in dispute, notably Kashmir. Some changes have taken place, such as the annexation by India of the former French and Portuguese holdings in India, and the cession by Muscat and Oman of Gwadar to Pakistan in 1958; in addition, some of India's territory was taken by force by China in 1962 on the ground that the British had occupied and annexed it to India unlawfully in the time of China's weakness. The net result of these changes was that the territorial claims of the two nations slightly exceeded the total area of the old undivided India. Modern India claims 1,261,309 square miles, which is somewhat more than one third the size of the United States. Pakistan claimed 365,529 square miles in 1961, an area larger than that of France, West Germany, East Germany, and Switzerland combined. Of the two parts, West Pakistan was much the larger, having 310,403 square miles in 1961 while East Pakistan, which is now the new nation Bangladesh, had only 55,126 square miles in 1961 but was the more populous.

A basic feature of life in the subcontinent since partition has been the growth in population. The first census of the two nations after independence was taken in 1951. At that time the population of India was about 356.9 million and that of Pakistan 75.7 million, making a total for the subcontinent of 432.6 million. Each country had another census in 1961, when the population of India was 439.2 million and that of Pakistan 93.8 million, making a total of 533 million. Each nation had a census scheduled for 1971. . . . [In that year] the Census Commissioner of India released a preliminary estimate subject to final computation, which gave a figure of 547 million, an increase in twenty years of 190 million (53.5 percent). An official estimate of the Pakistani population for 1970 gave a figure of about 114.2 million persons. Of this, West Pakistan, now all that is left of Pakistan, was estimated to have 53.5 million; East Pakistan, now Bangladesh, 60.7 million. *Bangladesh* (a government publication) in the issue of June 2, 1972, gave an estimate of 75 million. These figures are obviously not final. Bangladesh suffered severe losses of population in 1970-1972 because of natural calamities, slaughter of civilians by (West) Pakistan army forces, and flight of population as refugees from the terror of military repression. But for lack of any better figures we may assume that the total population of the subcontinent is now at least 661 million, which is more than the combined population of the United States, the Soviet Union, Great Britain, East and West Germany, France, Belgium, the Netherlands, and Switzerland. Among the world's nations the population of the subcontinent is exceeded only by that of China, which was estimated in 1969 to be 740 million. The United Nations *Bulletin of Statistics* for April 1971 estimated that by the year 2000 China would have 1.165 billion persons and India 1.084 billion; the total for the subcontinent as a whole would then presumably exceed that of China. At present there live in the subcontinent between one sixth and one fifth of the world's estimated population, occupying, however, less than 3 percent of the world's land area, excluding the polar regions.

The increase in population, though it shows that the subcontinent has steadily become able to support an ever increasing population, has not yet been accompanied by a satisfactory solution to the problem of providing an adequate food supply. The economy of each nation remains weak. Poverty is general, and sudden disaster can produce a famine, local or widespread according to the circumstances. The subcontinent lives today, as it has always lived, on the basis of agriculture, with relatively little supplement from industry. The imbalance is shown by the small number of industrial workers. The industrial labor force (that is, those employed in registered factories) amounts to around 5.5 million persons. This is probably less than 2 percent of the total labor force.

When traveling in the subcontinent one emerges suddenly from one of the few large cities to proceed for hundreds of miles across open country consisting of fields interspersed with uncultivated, or uncultivable, land, dotted with drab little villages, lightened only by an occasional whitewashed Hindu shrine or a Muslim mosque. Here and there one comes to a small town. There is nowhere any section to compare with the Atlantic coastal stretch in the United States of almost continuous urbanization from Portland, Maine, to Washington, D.C., or with some other American industrial areas, as around Pittsburgh and Chicago. According to official estimates only about 19.87 percent of the Indians, 22 percent of the people in Pakistan, and 13.1 percent in Bangladesh live in cities or town clusters of more than 100,000. (In the United States in 1970 more than two thirds of the population lived in central cities and Standard Metropolitan Statistical Areas.) Just as there are few cities and towns on the subcontinent, so too there are few isolated rural dwellings like the farmhouses of the United States. Most of the people (about two thirds) live in the more than 650,000 villages, which are settlements of generally less than five thousand population, averaging about six hundred. Of the villagers much the greater part (about 70 percent of the total population) cultivate the adjacent land; the others supply services or pursue handicrafts (such as weaving, pottery, metal work, oil pressing). The country, as one sees it, consists of clusters or even long stretches of tiny fields, bounded by low mud borders or thorn hedges, streaked with inarable land or jungle. Except at a few centers like Calcutta, Bombay, Madras, Jamshedpur, Asansol, Ahmedabad, Kanpur (Cawnpore), Sholapur, Karachi, and Lahore, factory chimneys are solitary or absent. This is how things are in cultivated sections of "the plains." In the hills and mountains, where agriculture is more difficult, villages are fewer and smaller. In the deserts, as in Rajasthan, they are still scarcer, though sometimes surprisingly large, and even cities are found, as at Bikaner and Jaisalmer.

The water necessary for agriculture is in most parts of the subcontinent of uncertain supply, and getting water is a perennial problem. When the annual monsoons are good the urgency of the problem is reduced, though much human labor is involved in getting the water to the fields. In a region where great rivers can be used for irrigation, as in the Punjab or Sind, the water is impounded by huge dams or barrages and led off through canals. The major outlets are large; from these run off smaller canals, and from these still smaller ones, and so by graduated decrease until the water finally reaches the fields through capillary-like distribution. For part of the year many of these channels must be cut off, to save the water until it is needed later. In dry spells peasants are busy throughout the day opening the sluices leading to their land so as to get the maximum flow during the hours

for which they have contracted and to direct the water first
to one part of their holdings and then to another. This is
the easiest of the subcontinent's ways of using human labor
to water the fields, and the most certain. In north India and
what was West Pakistan irrigation systems can use rivers
fed by the melting snows of the Himalayas and the rain that
falls upon their southern ranges during the summer monsoon. River-based irrigation is also practiced in other parts
of the subcontinent. Since independence, new schemes of irrigation have been inaugurated, many drawing their water
from rivers which are not fed by the Himalayan snows. Still
other schemes are under construction or are planned. The
flow of water in the rivers fluctuates from year to year, but
in no year does it cease entirely. Hence, peasants who live
in regions where there are river-fed irrigation systems are
usually better off and less subject to crop failure and famine
than those who must rely upon other sources.

In many areas the farmer gets water for his fields from a
well. In the north he may use a great Persian wheel, filling
the air with an interminable creaking as it dips an endless
chain of earthenware pots into the water, raises them above
ground level, and empties them into a trough from which
the water flows through runlets to the land. A blindfolded
camel or a pair of bullocks operate the mechanism, treading
a tiny circle all day long while a man or boy stands by to
keep them moving. Elsewhere a peasant may use a buffalo
or a pair of bullocks to raise and then lower a leather sack
into the water. There is a ramp built up to the well, rising
above its mouth some six feet or more. Along it the bullocks
tread forward and backward, relaxing the rope to which the
sack is tied and so letting it fall, then, when they reverse,
raising it to the wooden crossbeam at the high end of the
incline, where it is emptied into a channel to flow away. It
takes one man to empty the sack, another to drive the bullocks. Very poor peasants who own no bullocks and cannot
arrange to use those of a neighbor may operate such a well

with only human labor, the subcontinent's cheapest commodity, drawn from the ranks of the family.

In still other areas peasants raise the water with a sweep, like an Egyptian *shaduf*. This is a seesaw-like apparatus with a leather sack or an earthenware pot at one end of the beam and a counterpoise balanced at the other. All day long a man may walk back and forth along the beam, first lowering the container into the well and then raising it to the top, where another man empties it into a runway. Or at the extremity of the sweep there may be a bamboo pole with the vessel fastened to its end. A man stands beside the well forcing the pole down until the vessel is submerged, then letting it go so that the counterpoise can raise it to the surface. In south India one may see a channel or ditch full of water, into which two peasants, often women, jointly dip a shallow scoop, rhythmically swinging it back and forth between them, lifting the water and emptying it into a higher channel through which it flows to the fields.

Throughout most of the land there are hundreds of thousands of "tanks," or artificial ponds, which are filled by the annual rains and serve in the dry season for irrigation, washing, even drinking. It is important to keep these tanks in good working order. Silt must not be left to accumulate; plants, such as the rapidly spreading water chestnut, must be prevented from choking them and absorbing the water supply. A tank has to be cleaned out regularly, and with great care not to dig out the bottom and let the water seep away.

In south India there are myriads of such artificial storage ponds, varying in size from one acre or less to a square mile or more. At the lower end of a gentle slope is an earthen dike, which has to be kept in constant repair; the upper end is a marsh. Seen from the air, the country sparkles with them like the embroidered garments inset with bits of glass that women wear in Cutch. This method of maintaining agriculture appears to have been used since megalithic times.

In every part of the subcontinent where rice is cultivated, from the extreme south to the steep mountains of Kashmir, the peasants have made the cultivable land into series of terraces. These are broad where the slope of the ground is gradual, becoming narrow strips on the steep sides of the lower Himalayas. Around each terrace is a mud wall to retain the water that accumulates during the annual rains or is introduced by some device of irrigation.

Water brought by river or rainfall has always exercised a decisive influence on the life of the subcontinent. It has been responsible for the population concentrations, for the direction of ethnic invasions, for the development of the arts of civilization. Its importance is certified from the time of India's earliest literature. In the *Rig Veda*'s [an epic of Indian classical literature] myth of creation the cosmic Waters were at first confined by malevolent inertia and had to be released by a hero-god in fierce battle before a universe could exist and operate. In that same work and in allied literature are charms which priests recited to wake the aestivating frogs so that with the magic spells of their croaking they might summon the needed rain. Fifteen hundred years later the Sanskrit poets were extolling as divine music the peacock's cry, so shrill to our ears, that heralds the approach of the rainy season. In the . . . miniature paintings of the eighteenth and nineteenth centuries the musical mode appropriate to the rolling thunder and serpent-like streaks of lightning that accompany the vitalizing downpour of the moonsoon evokes the artist's most delicate powers of imagination.

What are the facts about the subcontinent's topography, its fertile plains, its river systems, its mountainous areas, its deserts, its basic water supply?

The subcontinent is shaped roughly like a quadrangle—or, more precisely, like a pentagon, though the fifth side is disproportionately short. One long point of the figure is the Deccan peninsula projecting sharply southward into the Indian Ocean, with the Arabian Sea on its west and the Bay

of Bengal on its east. The rest is mountainbound. Along the
northwestern side, now held by Pakistan, is a protective bar-
rier of hills and desert, generally difficult for armies or peoples on the trek, yet penetrable at various points, and providing the chief means of ingress to the subcontinent by
land throughout recorded history. The northern side is a
concave arc of lofty mountains, containing the world's highest peaks. It bars both the peoples and the cold winds of the
land beyond and at the same time blocks the rainclouds of
India from reaching Central Asia, where in consequence
large areas remain desert. These ranges are geologically
young and they and the nearby plains are disturbed by frequent tremors and occasional disastrous earthquakes, such
as those in Bihar in 1934 and Assam in 1950. On the east
the short fifth side is the Burma frontier, whose jungle-cov-
ered mountains are all but impassable.

Inside the northwestern and northern walls is the great
plain of the subcontinent. It extends from the peninsula of
Kathiawar in the present Republic of India beside the Arabian Sea, in a direction slightly west of north to Sind in
Pakistan; thence a little east of north for about seven hundred miles to the Himalayas, including all of Pakistan except some mountain areas. From here it turns eastward into
India below the curve of the Himalayan chain, across the
breadth of the country, coming to an end against the hills
of Assam and Bangladesh and the coast of the Bay of Bengal.

This plain varies from 80 to 200 miles in width. In its
sweeping extent it contains the greatest of the subcontinent's
river systems. In the west is the Indus, which rises on the
northern side of Himalayas, flows westward behind them to
round their end, separating them from the Karakoram and
Hindu Kush ranges and then drives inside the northwestern
frontier down to the sea. The Indus is fed by the five rivers
of the Punjab (Land of Five Streams), one of which (the
Sutlej) also rises north of the Himalayas not far from the
source of the Indus, but, unlike it, finds a route directly
through them. The four others (Jhelum, Chenab, Ravi,

Beas) rise in the range and flow directly to the lowlands. In the upper Punjab the moderate rainfall and the irrigation based upon its rivers support an extensive agriculture. Farther south, in the lower Punjab and Sind, rainfall is scanty, varying from ten to twenty inches annually and in many places being even less. Here agriculture is impossible except with the aid of irrigation. This has been practiced for millennia, but never on a scale to support a large population. Today there are vast systems of irrigation in this region, and others are under construction or planned. East of the long course of the Indus is the Great Indian Desert, which has neither rivers nor rainfall. In form it is an irregular triangle with one side paralleling the river and the others forming an apex which points eastward into Rajasthan in India. Southeast of Sind in India is Kathiawar, a region with moderate rainfall but enough to support a population of medium density.

The northern part of the Great Indian plain, often called Hindustan, contains the Ganges-Yamuna (Jamna or Jumna) river system, which only a low rise of ground separates from the Indus system. The soil of this region is a deep alluvial deposit. Its two main rivers, the Ganges and the Jumna, rise on the lower side of the Himalayas and curve southeast in gradually converging arcs until they unite at Allahabad. From there, absorbing many tributaries, the Ganges continues eastward to Bengal, where it is joined by the Brahmaputra. This last, like the Indus and the Sutlej, rises on the northern side of the Himalayas but, as though to polarize the Indus, flows eastward to turn and circle the eastern end of the mountain chain, where it finds an opening, reverses itself, and flows southwest. It and the Ganges unite and form an immense delta. Their waters reach the Bay of Bengal through many mouths, steadily depositing silt, and today, as for millennia in the past, continually projecting the land area into the bay as low flatland, subject from time to time to floods from the rivers or to tidal waves from the Bay of Bengal created by violent storms.

The part of the northern plain east of the Punjab, favored by its rivers, is in normal years also watered by seasonal rains. It is agriculturally the most desirable part of the subcontinent and has always been the goal of invaders entering from the passages of the northwest. The population density of this region is eight hundred to the square mile; it contains about two fifths of the subcontinent's inhabitants, although only about one sixth of the total area.

Below the northern plain is a complex highland, the upper end of which is embraced by the two extremes of the plain. Along its northern part are various ranges of low hills, of which the highest peak, Mount Abu, is 5,650 feet in elevation. The terrain of central India makes it a difficult area to traverse, and permits it to support only a moderately dense population. Indian literature has for 2,500 years spoken fearfully of the wild jungles and the primitive peoples in this area. The largest range of its hills is the Vindhyas, south of which is the Narmada (Narbada, Nerbudda) River. South of this are other ranges (of which the Satpura is the most important), and still farther south is the Tapti River. These two streams run from the center of the Indian peninsula westward to the Arabian Sea and are the only ones of the subcontinent's large rivers flowing in that direction.

Still farther south is the part of the plateau known specifically as the Deccan (South), which comprises most of the triangle of peninsular India. This tableland (varying from about 1,000 to 2,500 feet in elevation) tilts gently from west to east. Its great rivers rise on the western side, flow eastward across it, and empty in the Bay of Bengal. It is not well watered, either by streams or by rainfall, and much of its area is rocky or has soil of inferior quality. Nevertheless it supports around 250 persons to the square mile.

The Deccan is bordered on east and west by low ranges of mountains known as Ghats (Steps). The Western Ghats, a kind of seaboard scarp, which have a few peaks of approximately five thousand feet but average round three thousand feet, descend in thickly forested, bold declivities to the al-

luvial seaboard. The southern part of this shoreline, known
as the Malabar coast, is one of the best-watered, most fertile,
and most thickly populated parts of India, having around
1,300 persons to the square mile. On the other side of the
peninsula the discontinuous Eastern Ghats, averaging about
1,500 feet in altitude, are less picturesque. They lead down.
to another well-watered, productive, and thickly inhabited
alluvial plain, wider than that on the west and known as
the Coromandel coast. The central plateau terminates southward in clusters of hills called the Nilgiris (Blue Mountains)
and Palni, which respectively have peaks as high as 8,640
and 8,841 feet. Finally, below these, at the extreme south,
are the Cardamon Hills. Beyond these last is Cape Comorin,
the southernmost point of India, east and south of which
lies the fragrant island of Ceylon [now called Sri Lanka].

The Deccan highland is geologically old in comparison
with the Himalaya; hence its worn appearance and low elevation, though Hindu myth assigns a different reason. The
Vindhya mountain, says the great Sanskrit epic *Mahabharata,*
became jealous of Himalaya and elevated himself, intending
to surpass the latter and to interrupt the circuit of the sun
and moon around Mount Meru, the mythical crest peak of
the Himalayas and the assembly point of all the divine
beings. The gods were alarmed but handled the problem by
appealing for help to the renowned sage Agastya. He asked
Vindhya to give him passage to the south so that he might
carry civilization there, as he is traditionally credited with
doing, and Vindhya graciously assented, bowing himself low
and promising to remain so until the reverend sage should
return. But Agastya never came back, and Vindhya, true to
his promise, has never raised himself or even stirred. Being
old and settled, Vindhya, unlike the youthful Himalaya, is
free of earthquakes; it is not only lowly but resigned as well.

The most important climatic feature of the subcontinent
is the annual southwest monsoon, which brings "the rains,"
and gives India 90 percent of its heaven-dispensed water. So
impressive has this phenomenon been upon India's con-

sciousness that in her languages the commonest words for *year* primarily mean *rain* or *rainy season*. The southwest monsoon generally blows during the four months of June through September, when the high sun heats the land rapidly and the hot air rises so that a low-pressure area is created and cool air flows inland from the sea. As it comes in from across the Indian Ocean, it is laden with moisture which it has sucked up. One arm of the monsoon strikes the hills of the lower western (Malabar) coast of India, rises, cools off, and precipitates its water heavily. But by the time it has crossed the Western Ghats, it has lost most of its moisture and has little left to precipitate upon the Deccan behind them. Northerly along this coast the indrawn winds dispense their water in smaller and smaller amounts as the Ghats become lower, until they deposit scarcely any when they reach Cutch (Kach, Kutch) just below the Tropic of Cancer, and Sind, which the clouds hasten across, hoarding their treasure for Kashmir seven hundred miles to the north. Hence Gujarat, which is the region north of Bombay, is productive, rich, and thickly settled, but beyond it Cutch, Sind, Rajasthan, and parts of the Punjab, being almost rainless, are dry and thinly peopled except where irrigated from the Indus system.

The other arm of this monsoon rounds the southern end of India and Ceylon and proceeds north up the Bay of Bengal. It strikes the eastern coast unevenly, but gives fair coverage to the coastal plain lying between the Eastern Ghats and the Bay. When it gets to the head of the Bay of Bengal, it fans out to west, north, and east. The winds which blow westward water the inland areas of eastern India and the long northern plain of Bengal, Bihar, Uttar Pradesh, and the Punjab. They reach also into the center of the country. As they proceed westward, they steadily lose moisture until very little is left for the upper Punjab, especially the part which lies in Pakistan. They beat against the length of the first ranges of the Himalayas, rising and cooling and exhausting their last moisture on the Himalayas' southern side. The rainfall in northern India, in the years when it is sufficiently abundant, soaks the deep alluvial soil and fills the streams, which in the dry season are but thin trickles in wide sandy beds, transforming them into roaring floods. For the time the plain becomes a mass of fertile mud.

The currents of the monsoon which go to the north, northeast, and east drench East Bengal and Assam, especially the hills in Assam, which have the world's heaviest rainfall. Over eight hundred inches have been recorded in a single year. . . . This heavy precipitation fits the slopes of the mountains for tea gardens.

Supplementing the monsoon in areas of low elevation is the summer convectional rainfall when the heated earth sends up drafts of warm air, which create cumulus clouds that refresh their parent earth with gentle showers.

Additional rain comes to certain parts of the subcontinent during the months of November and December, when breezes blow inland following the retreating southwest monsoon; sometimes these are called the northeast monsoon. Over most of the country these winds are dry, with only occasional light rainfall known as mango showers. They make the winter season in northern India a time of cool weather with almost unbroken sunshine and a comfortable temperature, ideal for tourists but of no help to the peasant if the southwest monsoon has been deficient and his crops need water. In South India the case is different. The part of the northeast monsoon which comes inland from across the Bay of Bengal carries moisture which it has absorbed from that body of water. It precipitates and waters the coastal plain and succeeds in carrying some of its charge across the low Eastern Ghats into the rest of Andhra and Tamil Nadu, and into Mysore. With this supplement to the rainfall of the southwest monsoon the area is able to support a good deal of intensive agriculture. Nevertheless, neither monsoon brings the region just east of the Western Ghats very heavy rainfall, and each monsoon is fickle. There is no certainty of adequate annual rain to guarantee full crops, and often there is short supply and the area may be in difficulty.

If "the rains," that "annual gamble" from the southwest, are "normal" and widespread, the subcontinent is prosperous. That is, there is no serious food shortage; the government can collect the land revenue; the peasantry do not have to borrow from the village moneylenders at a ruinous rate of interest and may even do something toward reducing the principal of their debts. But if the rains are scanty in any area or fail, not only do the fields get no direct water from heaven; the sources of irrigation dwindle too. Rivers fall, may even dry up; the village tanks (ponds) are not replenished; the water table is lowered and wells go dry. On the other hand, if in northern India the rains are too full and the rivers flood, as in 1950, 1960, 1971, seed may be washed out, cattle carried off, villages destroyed, and ruin comes upon the area and the peasantry. Where there is irrigation from snow-fed streams, as in the Punjab, the case is not so desperate, for the mountain slopes always get a share of rain, which ultimately collects in the rivers. Elsewhere the inevitable result is poor crops or none at all. Agriculture stops; food is exhausted; there follows a declaration of shortage, distress, scarcity, or famine, and relief must be brought in from outside. Such conditions have been reported since about the beginning of the third century B.C., when as we are told in the tradition of the Jains, the leaders of their faith left Bihar and went south to Mysore to stay until a twelve-year famine came to an end; this was the way in which Jainism came to south India, where a part of the Jain community still exists and has its monuments. Probably no one can imagine the full horror of a famine-stricken region unless he has seen it. The report of this twelve-year famine comes from shortly after the beginning of documented history in the subcontinent, and famines have been reported ever since. The inevitability of famine, unless provision is made in advance to meet it, is one of the deepest concerns to the subcontinent. After the partition of India the rival claims of India and Pakistan to irrigation waters of the Indus system led to one of the most serious quarrels between the two nations, which was settled only in 1960.

Though the subcontinent is an agricultural area with about 82 percent of its crops in food, it still does not raise all the food it eats. This is true even in a year when the rains are good. In prepartition times it imported from 1.5 million to 2.5 millions tons of rice annually from Burma; lack of that rice when the Japanese occupied Burma during World War II was one of the causes of the Bengal famine of 1943. India is more dependent upon food imports than Pakistan, and obtains food grains today under allotments from the Food and Agriculture Organization. Pakistan, on the other hand, is a wheat-growing surplus area, and in most years has a small amount to export.

Complicating the problem of feeding human beings is the presence of a large animal population. The subcontinent in 1945 had 170 million cows and 46 million buffaloes, about 44 million sheep and 56 million goats, and many camels (1.9 million), horses (1.8 million), and donkeys (1.9 million). Postpartition figures are not available for Pakistan, but in 1966 (provisional estimate) India alone had 176 million cattle, 52.9 million buffaloes, 42 million sheep, 64.5 million goats, 1.1 million horses. Orthodox Hindus do not eat the flesh of these, though the unorthodox may eat mutton or goat's flesh, and Muslims eat meat when they can afford it. These animals, therefore, do not relieve India's food needs much, except by providing dairy products. Even this they do only scantily and in poor quality—hence Indians, who at all ages are fond of milk, on visiting the United States exclaim at the abundance and the excellence of the milk everywhere on sale. Fishing is relatively undeveloped in the subcontinent and except in a few areas, such as Bengal, contributes little to food resources.

The chief food crops of the subcontinent and their approximate annual production are: rice, about 47 million metric tons; wheat, about 20 million metric tons; lesser crops of millet, maize, pulses [edible seeds of legumes], spices, sugar cane; oilseeds, especially groundnuts (peanuts); also rape [plant of the mustard family whose seeds yield an oil and whose leaves are used for fodder], mustard, sesame. Of commercial crops there are produced about 6 million bales (400 lbs. each) of cotton; and 3 million metric tons of jute; 0.4 million tons of tobacco; about 700 million pounds of tea. Both India and Pakistan produce much wool for export.

The bulk of the village population gets only the most meager living in terms of food, clothing, and shelter. Urban factory labor lives no better, possibly worse. Without seeing Indians in their villages, towns, and cities, it is difficult for a westerner to visualize the extent and effect of their poverty. Since 1952 the government of India has operated a Community Development Program to improve village living conditions, and has also done something less ambitiously planned to raise urban living standards. The accomplishments are in many cases impressive to long-time foreign residents in India who remember the conditions of village and urban life before independence, but of course are not noticed by new arrivals. In Pakistan less has been attempted and accomplished. If the average American visitor wants to remain sensitive to the conditions in which the masses of the people live, it is well for him not to stay in the country long. Very quickly the want, the disease, and the misery become only accepted facts.

In 1946 the government's Health Survey and Development Committee . . . reported the average individual diet figure to be 1,750 calories a day. The 1958 estimates of the Food and Agriculture Organization of the United Nations placed the per capita daily caloric intake of the subcontinent at around 2,050, well below the 2,250 or so which was the minimum requirement cited by the economist M. K. Bennett (*The World's Food*, 1954, especially pp. 189-212). This diet was found to be "ill balanced" as well as low, and it was estimated that 30 percent of India's families were undernourished. Before the Second World War, with food supply at "normal," the director of the Indian Medical Service . . . estimated that 41 percent of the people were "poorly nourished," that is, endured continued semistarvation. The government of India in 1952 said that its food deficit was 10 percent. A deficit still continued in 1961 in spite of the completion of two five-year plans of economic development, and the country was obliged to import substantial quantities of food. In 1972 the shortage still continued. Pakistan has also had to import food in spite of her five-year plans. It has always been the case in the subcontinent that when food supply increases in any area, the people breed up to consumption of the total supply at the old subsistence level. Instead of raising living standards, the result has been an increase in the number of people living in the old misery.

For clothing a gauge may lie in the consumption of cotton textiles—almost all clothing on the subcontinent is of cotton. The per capita consumption in India for personal clothing and household purposes combined was about 14.32 yards in 1952; in 1962 it was about 16.26 yards. Figures given for the world consumption of textiles are 42 yards per person per year; for the United States, 64 square yards of cotton textiles alone.

Housing is equally inadequate. In the villages most dwellings are made of mud and wattle or sun-dried brick, crowded together in an irregular huddle, affording little protection from the winter cold, the burning heat of summer, and the torrents of the rainy season. The average floor space per person in the villages is impossible to determine. A survey in 1953-1954 showed that in fifty-three cities and towns 44 percent of the houses had only one room, 28 percent two rooms, 12 percent three rooms, 16 percent four or more rooms. In the large cities there exist crowded quarters sometimes with six or more persons to a cubicle, while one water spigot may have to provide for a whole neighborhood and latrines may be few and unsanitary. In some sections the quarters were without a chimney or a window, with no lights or water supply, and no sanitary arrangements. Con-

ditions can hardly be much better now, since living costs
have gone up more rapidly in intervening years than wages,
and the urban population has increased, while little new
housing has been erected. In every city there is a large number of people with no housing at all, who sleep each night
in the open.

In typical village and urban dwellings furniture scarcely
exists. A house, or hut, has a fireplace consisting of a few
bricks or stones or molded clay set to form three sides of a
rectangle over which a pot or pan can be placed; it usually
also contains a few metal cooking vessels and some primitive
implements for farming or the pursuit of a handicraft. That
is likely to be all. Scavenging is a function of the village dogs.
With these basic handicaps to health has gone heavy inci-
dence of disease and paucity of preventive and curative medicine. The various improvement projects have made only
little impression on these conditions.

The combined effect of poor diet, insufficient clothing,
substandard housing, and paucity of medical resources is a
high mortality rate. The 1941 census of (then undivided)
India gave a mortality figure of 21.8 per 1,000 (against 10.6
in the United States), but some critical studies of the data by
competent demographers set it much higher, that is, at 31.2
per 1,000. The 1951 census gave the rate in India 14.4 (again
possibly too low), and provisionally the estimate for 1957
was 11.0. Figures since then are also unreliable. . . . For the
decade 1951-1960, the registered death rate in India is given
in *India 1969* as 11, but the estimated rate is 41.7. In the
same source the registered birth rate is given as 22 and the
estimated rate as 41.7. Nevertheless, the increase of population shows that the death rate has been declining. Life expectation at birth, according to actuarial calculations published in the Indian census reports, averaged 32 years in
1951 (as against approximately 60 for whites and 48 for
blacks in the United States at the same time). In 1961 an
unofficial Indian calculation based on the 1961 census put it
at 42 (figures are not yet calculated for the 1971 census).

The brevity and ills of life in India have often been held responsible for her preoccupation with religion, emphasis upon family organization, and intense desire to have progeny and have it early in life, thus conducing to early marriage.

To meet the needs of expanding population both India and Pakistan have been using two approaches. One is to increase production. Attempts to expand agricultural output have involved developing enlarged irrigation schemes; producing new strains of food grains, which are more resistant to climate and give greater yield; establishing fertilizer factories; adopting improved agricultural techniques through use of better tools and now by introducing machinery as far as is practicable, that is, without displacing more agricultural laborers than the subcontinent can provide with other employment. Each country, and especially India, has also been expanding industry in many fields. In addition to efforts to increase economic production, each nation has been promoting programs of population control by the use of contraception; here, too, India has been having the greater success. . . .

For some five millennia man in the Indian subcontinent has not merely held his own against the disadvantages which nature puts upon him, but has searched out and utilized means to maintain a life of high achievement in the arts of civilization. If on the spiral of history South Asia once was more accomplished in those arts than the West but now is less so, it may again reach a position of equality. That, at least, is the hope of many citizens of the subcontinent. But the two nations started life after a wearying struggle to achieve independence, and a destructive conflict between Hindus and Muslims, the ill effects of which still continue. With no time granted for recuperation, they have had to attack their critical basic living problems, build new sources of national strength, and assume international responsibilities. Their resources and energy have not yet been equal to the demands, though there has been progress. With the creation of Bangladesh in 1972 the feeding of people became the first problem for three nations.

THE SUBCONTINENT: A DIFFERENT WORLD [3]

The countries of India, Pakistan [and Bangladesh], and Ceylon [Sri Lanka] stretch over an enormous land area. The subcontinent extends more than two thousand miles from the towering heights of the Himalaya Mountains in the far north to the tropical green jungles and golden beaches of the Indian Ocean in the south. It is about 2,500 miles from the western tip of . . . Pakistan to the eastern rim of India.

India and Pakistan [and Bangladesh] have much in common. They are poor, largely agricultural, and heavily populated. The island nation of Ceylon has a higher standard of living than the other . . . [three]. . . . [Today India has a population of more than 570 million, Pakistan more than 50 million, Bangladesh more than 60 million, Ceylon more than 12 million.] One out of every six people in the world today lives in the subcontinent.

At their present rates of population growth, the . . . [four] countries will have close to two times as many people by the year 2000 as they have now. One of their most serious problems is how to slow their population growth. If they do not, they will one day outgrow their food supply.

Another problem is also linked to population. This is how to raise living standards in India . . . Pakistan [and Bangladesh]. These standards remain among the lowest in the world, despite the progress of recent years. The rapid growth in the subcontinent's population means that any increase in food production is matched by the increased number of people. So there is not much more food available for each person than before.

[3] From *The Indian Subcontinent*, by Irwin Isenberg, UN official. Scholastic Book Services. '72. p 12+. Excerpts reprinted by permission from *The Indian Subcontinent*, by Irwin Isenberg, © 1972 by Scholastic Magazines, Inc.

India, Pakistan [and Bangladesh], and Ceylon share many customs, traditions, beliefs. These have grown out of thousands of years of history, and they have an important place in daily life. In fact, custom and tradition are so powerful they sometimes slow down or help halt the changes which could improve living conditions.

For example, in one region many new wells were put in to increase the water supply. These wells operated in a different way from the ones already in use. Government workers tried to tell the people how the new wells worked and to show that they produced more water than the old wells did. But the villagers were suspicious. They refused to use the new wells and even filled some with sand. Gradually, however, such attitudes are being overcome, and people are accepting new ways. But this may take generations, although the pace is quickening.

Even while sharing many customs and traditions, the . . . countries of the subcontinent show an astonishing degree of variety. Through more than four thousand years of history, they have developed different religions and cultures. These differences give each country its own personality and character.

Many contrasts can be seen. Some farmers use modern methods and machinery, but most continue to plow, plant, and harvest in ways that were old when Columbus discovered America. There are great cities with populations in the millions, but more than 80 percent of the people live in villages. Some of these little communities have not changed much in looks and habits for generations.

Architectural contrasts: Ornate stone temples chiseled by patient artists hundreds of years ago stand near villages of mud huts almost ready to collapse. In some cities, new highrise buildings have gone up near ancient monuments and ruins. Modern homes lie in the shadow of old palaces once inhabited by maharajahs rich beyond belief. Whole new cities are being built with the most advanced architectural ideas, and long-buried cities are being excavated and explored.

Literacy vs. ignorance: The subcontinent has fine universities and scientific institutes, but three people out of every four can neither read nor write. Tens of thousands of students have gone to Britain, the United States, and the Soviet Union to study, but hundreds of millions of villagers have never been more than a few miles from their birthplace.

West and East: Many city men wear western-type clothes, but women wear a variety of traditional garments. For most women of the subcontinent it would be unthinkable to wear a western-style dress. A few city teenagers dance together to rock music, but most young men and women have little contact with one another until they are married.

Language differences: English is spoken by educated people in all regions. This is a result of British domination of the subcontinent from the 1700s until after World War II. Then India and Ceylon won their independence, and Pakistan was created out of Indian territory. Most people, however, speak one of the subcontinent's fifteen major languages or one of its hundreds of dialects.

People in the northern and southern parts of the relatively small island of Ceylon use different languages. Citizens within some of India's various states cannot understand one another when each speaks his local language. Residents of . . . [Bangladesh and Pakistan] separated by almost a thousand miles of Indian territory, also speak different languages. . . .

Because of the subcontinent's size and diversity, no single book could discuss all aspects of life in each of the regions. Even villages just a few dozen miles apart may have contrasting ways. Between Pakistan in the north and Ceylon in the south are a wide range of living and working conditions and great differences in traditions and customs. . . .

A World Apart

India, Pakistan [and Bangladesh], and Ceylon are made up of many villages—more than . . . [600,000] in all. They range in population from a few hundred to a few thousand. Some are near large cities, but many are specks of habitation far from a bus stop or railway station. A few villages are relatively prosperous. But most are poor beyond imagination.

Many of these villages have no electricity, plumbing, sanitation, or schools. Still rarer are libraries, doctors, dentists, paved streets, movies, or phones. Mail reaches many villages very slowly. Few newspapers, magazines, or books reach them at all. Strangers rarely pass through. Little news from distant places filters in, even though nearly every village has at least one transistor radio.

Apart from holidays and ceremonies, village life is much the same, day in, day out. Perhaps a dancing group, a puppet show, or a magician may come to a village, especially to a large one. Once or twice a year a family may go to a fair for a day of shopping, visiting, and entertainment. Occasionally, people may go to another village to attend a wedding. In Ceylon the poverty is not so extreme, distances between towns are shorter, and contact is easier. There the villages do not seem so isolated.

Despite the poverty and lack of contact with the wider world, a village is actually a lively place. Early in the morning, just as the sun rises, the farmers walk to their fields. These are spread out on all sides of the village.

Village boys hurry cows, goats, and sheep out to pasture. A camel, with its load of grain bouncing at every step, moves slowly, like a ship gliding through the land. In the south, elephants in the forests help men move logs and clear the terrain.

Everybody carries everything, including small bundles, on his head rather than in his arms. A procession of men, carrying sacks of rice or bundles of straw on their heads, files past. A small boy runs along with a large stack of laundry on his head. Women and girls balance full water jugs on their heads as they walk quickly and gracefully home from the village well. The village well serves as a social center where friends meet and gossip.

During the day the main street of the village is busy. Small shops sell wheat, rice, sugar, salt, cloth. Women and children have carried bags of fruit from the family fields and placed them for sale by the side of the street. For the equivalent of a penny or two, one can buy a huge apple, a juicy mango, a papaya (which tastes like a soft cantaloupe), or an opened coconut. In the southern part of the subcontinent, nothing seems more refreshing on a hot day than cool coconut milk.

Cyclists pedal slowly along the street, weaving through knots of people. If the village is on a through road, a bus or car may drive past in a great cloud of dust. Its horn blares as it tries to make its way through the slow-moving people, buffaloes, cows, dogs, and chickens in the road.

Animals are always in the village streets. Pigs grunt about, eating garbage. Goats chew on leaves and bits of vegetables dropped from carts or stalls. Cows, buffaloes, and dogs, with a scattering of men and boys, lie drowsing in the shade. In India, ... the cows ... are considered sacred.

Here and there rows of round, flattened cow-dung patties lie drying in the sun or plastered on house walls. These patties are the major fuel for cooking fires. Wood is too scarce and charcoal too expensive.

The village itself is mud brown in color. Its twisting streets and lanes are formed of hard-packed earth. In larger villages the main street may be paved.

During the southwest *monsoon* (rainy season in the northern, central, and southwestern parts of India), the village becomes a swamp. The water is often ankle-deep. The southwest monsoon lasts from June to September. In southeastern India, the northeast monsoon produces the same effect in the winter months. During the dry season, every step kicks up a fine powder of dust. In the northern regions, the hot winds produce sandstorms.

The outer walls of the village houses border the lanes. These walls, made of hardened, unbaked mud bricks, are cracked by the sun and pitted by the rain. Framed wooden openings, entrances to the individual courtyards, are built at intervals along the brown walls. The homes of the rich may have carved wooden doors, and the walls around the door are painted white.

In some regions each house stands apart, but in many villages one house is built up against the next. In both northern and southern India most villages have a large pond or "tank," often with a temple built beside it. This, plus the wells, serves the community for washing, drinking, and bathing purposes.

Inside the walls is a courtyard. Some are large and shaded by trees. Most courtyards, however, are about twenty feet on each side. The courtyard rather than the house itself is the center of family activity. Here the women grind wheat, spread out rice to dry, and spin cotton. They prepare meals over an earthen stove in one corner. They spend much of their lives in the courtyard.

Neighbors gather to chat in the courtyard. Children play here all day long. Busy mothers put their older children in charge of the younger ones. A girl just nine or ten may carry her baby brother or sister on her hip for a good part of the day. If she is not looking after a child, she is drawing water from the well, helping with the crops, cleaning the house, or preparing the next meal with her mother.

At night the family's animals are kept in the courtyard, although some villages have central compounds for all the animals. Most villagers treat buffaloes and cows almost as members of the family because the farm labor of these animals is indispensable. The animals also give milk, which the family sells or uses itself. It is sometimes said that the loss of a child is a great sorrow, but the loss of a bullock is a calamity. This is because the family may not have enough money or credit to buy another animal.

At the rear of the courtyard stands the house itself. It usually has one floor and, like the outer walls, is made of sun-dried bricks, or, if the family can afford them, of fired bricks. Some houses have a coating of white plaster. Roofs are made of wooden beams or straw-covered bamboo and sealed with a layer of clay to keep the monsoon rain out.

In Ceylon and southern India, roofs are slanted and made of red tile. These give the village a neat and pleasant look. The houses of the poorest villagers are small tent-like layers of bamboo and straw placed over a framework of sticks.

If the family is relatively prosperous, its house has a narrow, covered veranda. Behind it are several small, dark, windowless rooms. In these rooms are clay pots or bins which hold grains such as wheat, maize (corn), or millet; vegetables such as beans; and *ghee* (or *ghi*), a butter product. Clothing and blankets are stored in chests or hung from wall pegs. Many brides receive large three-legged brass or brass-plated containers in which they keep their best clothes.

Family valuables, such as money or pieces of jewelry, are hidden in holes in the floor or walls. The hiding place is necessary because there are no banks in the villages. Some women wear all the jewelry they own. They do not want to risk leaving it in the house. Wearing their jewelry is also a way of letting others know how wealthy they are. Even if they do not wear all of it, village women are often adorned with six or eight silver bracelets on each ankle, several toe rings, arm bangles of gold or silver (or, among poorer people, of glass), a neck chain, and perhaps a gold or silver nose ring.

Many village streets are very dirty. But the people try hard to keep their homes as clean as possible. Floors are washed down and swept every day, sometimes twice daily. The entire house is frequently gone over with a fresh coat of mud to fill cracks or repair sections that have begun to crumble. On holidays the women use a rice paste to paint designs on the walls and door. These designs are supposed to bring good fortune and to ward off evil.

During the chillier winter months in northern India (December through February), the family sleeps on straw mats in the inner rooms. Some prefer to sleep around the fire kept burning all night in the courtyard. As the weather warms, everyone moves out-of-doors to sleep.

During the summer months . . . the temperature goes up to 115 degrees during the day and does not drop much below 100 degrees at night. . . . In much of the subcontinent, summer heat is so extreme it becomes difficult to move around during the middle of the day. The house becomes an oven, a person's body sags, and there is no way to escape the fierce heat.

The house is almost bare of furniture. Often the only piece is a lightweight woven rope cot, called a *charpoy* (four legs), used as a bed at night. During the day, the *charpoy* stands on end or serves as a lounge or chair. Two or three people can easily sit cross-legged on it.

Some families have wooden chairs, but these are not for everyday use. They are reserved for honored male guests or for the most solemn occasions. The interior rooms may also have mirrors, a small wooden table, and perhaps posters with religious themes.

Despite the poverty of most villagers, a visitor is always welcome in their homes. He will be offered a wooden chair, the family's own or a borrowed one, as a sign of respect.

Soon the guest will be brought a plate of fruits and a glass of warm buffalo milk sweetened with sugar. Later he will be given a large meal prepared especially for him. However, he will eat only with the men of the family. The women in the household usually eat by themselves after the men have finished. In some regions, the women prepare no extra food for themselves, but eat only what the men have left.

East Meets West

The subcontinent's largest cities—Calcutta, Bombay, Delhi, Madras, and Hyderabad in India; Karachi [and] Lahore . . . in Pakistan [and Dacca in Bangladesh]—have two personalities.

One is modern. The cities have new office buildings and hotels. Wide boulevards carry more automobile traffic each year. Large apartment buildings and housing developments have shot up. Suburbs have spacious homes set in gardens ablaze with flowers. The cities and the suburbs also have large numbers of more modest houses for middle-income families.

Department stores in the cities sell a wide variety of goods. In or near the cities of India and Pakistan are great industrial complexes. These textile mills, steel plants, and machinery factories employ thousands and use the newest equipment. Ceylon has only one really large city, Colombo. Its industrial development is not as far along as [that] in the most advanced areas of India and Pakistan.

But the cities also have another personality. Forts, palaces, temples, and shrines that are hundreds of years old lie scattered throughout many of them. New Delhi, India's capital, is built next to Delhi, which is a series of old cities. Delhi's ancient communities hold more than a thousand monuments of the past—some of them in near-perfect condition. These age-old buildings give the modern viewer some idea of the glory and magnificence of India's ancient civilizations.

For instance, in Delhi is a great palace inside a huge three-hundred-year-old complex of buildings known as the Red Fort. A high, thick, red sandstone wall with an intricate gateway surrounds the complex. One of these rooms has ceilings and walls of inlaid glass. Other walls were once studded with semiprecious stones. There were elaborate fountains, marble canals, and exquisite gardens. In the old days, dancing girls, perhaps as many as a hundred at a time, performed at night at the emperor's command. Musicians played, poets recited, and learned men told of ancient times and great battles.

Scented water ran in the baths. Delicious food odors hung lightly in the air. It must have been a scene of splendor that can scarcely be imagined today. On one of the walls was inscribed in the Persian language in golden letters:

> If there is a paradise on earth,
> It is here! It is here! It is here!

The subcontinent's most famous monument is the Taj Mahal in the city of Agra. The Taj was built more than three hundred years ago by an emperor as a tomb for his wife. (*Taj Mahal,* named in her memory, means *distinguished one of the palace.*) Made of white marble by an army of laborers at a staggering cost, the Taj Mahal is one of the world's most beautiful buildings. As seen by moonlight, its perfect proportions reflected in the long pool of water before it, the Taj Mahal is a shimmering vision that casts a magic spell.

The Ceylonese town of Anuradhapura was once the capital of a great empire. Dozens of huge buildings and stone carvings completed as many as two thousand years ago are reminders of its shadowy past. This city was once famous throughout the ancient world for the beauty of its buildings and the splendor of its art.

It is not only through monuments by which the old world lives on in the subcontinent. The full flavor of this old world can best be experienced by a walk through one of the bazaar (shopping) areas in the old part of any large city. In Delhi, Chandni Chowk—"the square of moonlight" —is the main street of the biggest bazaar. Once it was a wide avenue down which emperors and princes rode on elephants with jeweled trappings. Now it is a crowded jumble of stores, people, and vehicles.

Many small streets lead from Chandni Chowk. Lanes and alleys branch from these side streets, and passageways seemingly without end stem from the alleys. As a visitor walks deeper into the winding, narrow, crowded streets of the bazaar, he may feel that he can never find his way out.

Three- and four-story buildings line the streets of the bazaar. The upper floors are divided into small apartments which house big families. Shops occupy the ground floors. Most of the shops are very small, perhaps ten to twelve feet wide and only a little deeper. Some may even be just four or five feet wide and a few feet deep.

The shop's owner sits cross-legged on a waist-high shelf. His stock of goods—combs, sunglasses, ball point pens—is piled up next to him. In a larger store, the owner often sits cross-legged on a wooden floor or on a raised platform covered with a white cotton cloth. Customers may sit on the platform with him and drink a cup of tea or coffee while making a purchase.

It is said that if someone looks long enough he can find anything he wants in the bazaar. There are ivory markets with carved figures of animals and Hindu gods and goddesses; brass markets; gem shops with sapphires, garnets, topazes, and moonstones; bamboo shops; trinket shops with thousands of inexpensive arm and leg bracelets; book stalls; miniature foundries where men sweat over tiny blast furnaces as they handle red-hot pieces of metal; and bicycle repair sheds —all stretching out for block after block in noisy, colorful confusion.

One street is entirely filled with the shops of silversmiths. Another street has shops with beautiful carpets. Other shops are filled with great bolts of red, purple, gold, and green cottons and silks. Next to a cloth store is a tailor's shop where three men sit on straw mats. They are bent over their hand-powered sewing machines, carefully tailoring cloth into clothing. Another tailor is measuring a customer for a suit.

The art of bargaining reaches its height in the bazaar. When expert bargainers, who love a contest, confront each other, the purchase of an article is a long and delicate matter. The buyer doesn't simply ask the price and pay the first such price named. It is accepted that this figure is inflated and is merely the opening round. When the customer hears the first price, he offers half. The shopkeeper looks pained. He protests that his original price was already low, a special concession to the customer. Then the merchant quotes a figure somewhat lower than his first one.

Now it is the customer's turn to look pained. He claims that he can get the same article in a nearby store for much less—and he offers a bit more than he did before. After some minutes, perhaps including an interval when the customer indicates he is ready to walk out, a price will be agreed upon. The more expensive the item, the more subtle and prolonged the bargaining process. But not to bargain would be to miss half the challenge.

In the bazaar are tiny food counters with steaming pots of potatoes, rice and beans cooking over charcoal fires. In butcher shops, men are slicing meat with knives held between their toes. Fruit stalls are piled high with apples, oranges, raisins, bananas. Candy stands have syrupy sugar balls that dissolve in the mouth, and candies made with milk, sugar, and nuts. Some are covered with real silver so fine that it can be eaten.

In one place, a barber is squatting on the sidewalk, his tools spread out before him on a small cloth. Squatting opposite him is a customer, whom he is carefully shaving with a curved razor that looks like a small sickle. When he completes the shave, the barber snips his customer's finger and toe nails. Then the barber rubs oil vigorously into his customer's hair and over the bared upper half of his body.

All the while the two men continue to squat. This is a position most westerners find hard to endure for more than a few minutes. The people of the subcontinent, however, can squat for an hour or more and not feel any strain. Many say they find it more comfortable to squat than to sit.

In a nearby lane, shoemakers are at work on the sidewalk. At the corner a man sits before a stock of peanuts heated by a fire in a small pot. He sells the peanuts in tiny bags, or small containers of leaves pinned together, for about a penny a bag.

Next to the peanut seller is an old woman who looks seventy, though she could just as well be less than fifty. Her face is wrinkled, her hair white, her teeth missing, her feet bare, her ankles and wrists covered with bracelets, her body wrapped in a long piece of faded cloth. She is sitting before a pile of green bananas for sale. Beside her a naked child, perhaps her grandson, lies asleep.

Crowds are everywhere. The streets are noisy with children playing tag, jumping rope, spinning tops. Women are washing clothes in front of water pumps. Usually they scrub each piece and then pound it on a broad flat stone to beat out all the dirt. There are few washing machines in the subcontinent.

Trying to make their way through the bazaar are moving vehicles of every kind. It is said that Chandni Chowk is the site of the world's most tangled traffic jam. The streets are choked with cars, busses, taxis, scooters, tricycles, three-wheeled scooters with seats, horse-drawn carriages, buffalo-drawn carts, wandering animals. Sometimes a cow will lie down in the middle of a narrow street. No one forces the cow to move; rather, the traffic must squeeze itself around the cow. Sometimes people on the sidewalks must also give way to cows.

II. THE PEOPLE: HOW THEY LIVE

EDITOR'S INTRODUCTION

In order to know something of the subcontinent, it is necessary to have some understanding of its values and attitudes, which for the most part are quite alien to Westerners. In largely rural societies which guard their traditions carefully and in which change occurs slowly if at all, values and attitudes are often those shaped centuries ago.

This is the world of the caste system (in India) and rigidly stratified social layers in which every man has an exact place; of arranged marriages in which bride and groom may have met only once briefly prior to the wedding; of women living their lives in seclusion (in Pakistan and Bangladesh) and never exposing their faces to any male except those in their immediate families; of the joint family system in which several generations live communally; of work methods unchanged in some cases for five hundred years; and of subsistence living for hundreds of millions of people.

The first article describes the origins and present status of the caste system in India. It should be noted that while the Indian government is officially committed to the abolition of the worst excesses of the caste system, caste practices are still strong in the villages, where some 80 percent of the people live. It should also be noted that in past centuries the caste system provided, to some extent, a rational organization for living and surviving in a difficult environment.

The next article speaks of the isolation of women in Pakistan brought about by special circumstances, but in broader terms the article illustrates what *purdah* (or seclusion) means. Purdah as an institution has a strong hold on

Muslim life in the subcontinent, though it is breaking down among some members of the well-educated class.

The third article describes a particular phenomenon—the indifference of man toward his fellow man—which has often been observed in various parts of the subcontinent. The author argues that this indifference has resulted in a lack of social cohesion which has had serious consequences for national development.

The next selection examines India's seemingly endless troubles through the experiences and thoughts of a sidewalk vendor, a farmer, an industrialist, and a family-planning worker. Through their words the reader may gain a sense of the enormity of the problems facing the governments of the subcontinent.

The following extract offers a view of life in Karachi today. What is said about Karachi in Pakistan could also be said about most of the other large cities on the subcontinent. In fact, Calcutta in India is known to some as a city beyond hope. Deplorable conditions have arisen because of mass migration to the cities as a result of overcrowding in rural areas. The cities, in turn, lack the funds, the trained manpower, and often the motivation to cope with their constantly mounting problems.

The last article, more optimistic, suggests that through communications some progress can be made in stimulating people to help themselves and describes what one UN organization, UNICEF, is doing. At the same time, many other groups as well as the governments concerned, are trying to spark progress in a variety of fields. Yet, all of these efforts are necessarily small in relation to the overwhelming need.

THE CASTE SYSTEM [1]

Long centuries ago the Indian people began to divide into different groups, or classes. At first these were only

[1] From *The Indian Subcontinent*, by Irwin Isenberg, UN official. Scholastic Book Services. '72. p 114-20+. Excerpts reprinted by permission from *The Indian Subcontinent*, by Irwin Isenberg, © 1972 by Scholastic Magazines, Inc.

separate classes, without the caste codes which arose later.
Then the most powerful groups found a way to strengthen
and preserve their own privileges and position. At the top
was a group called Brahmans. These were the priests and
teachers. Next to the Brahmans were the statesmen and soldiers. Merchants and farmers made up the third. Common
laborers and workers (serfs) were in the fourth and lowest
group.

The first three groups are known even today as the
twice born. Boys in these castes pass through a special ceremony when they are ten. A priest anoints the boy with oil,
chants sacred verses, then ties a sacred thread around the
boy's body. He is now considered to have been born again.
The thread, a reminder of caste obligations, will be worn
until it rots away. Then it will be replaced many times
during the boy's life.

Each of the four groups once had a carefully worked-out
set of obligations and rights. The duty of the merchant and
farmer caste, for instance, was to engage in commerce and
trade and increase the wealth of the land. The ancient codes
instructed a member of this group to know "the prices of
mercantile commodities, especially of gems, pearls, coral,
iron, cloth, perfumes, and liquids. He must be skilled in
sowing seeds, in the qualities of land, in weights and measures, in the excellence and defects of articles of traffic, in
the advantages and disadvantages of different districts, in
the probable gain and loss on goods, in the breeding of cattle,
in the wages of servants, in the various languages of men, in
the best place for keeping cattle. . . ."

By about the third century B.C., when the caste system
began to take over the old four-class society, laws spelled out
the relations between the castes. In later centuries these
laws became a complex code. A Hindu could not marry
someone of another caste. Nor could he eat with a person of
a lower caste. It was equally forbidden for him to eat with
a person of a higher caste. Social functions such as weddings
could not be attended by people of different castes.

Seating was another important aspect of caste. One student of Indian customs wrote; "The height of a seat one occupies is in direct ratio to the social position of the occupant. A man of lower caste cannot sit in the presence of a man of higher caste. Men of the same caste, but having different social positions on account of differences in wealth or on account of some prejudice, may sit in one another's presence, but the lesser man must be careful to occupy a lower seat than his superior. If seats of the correct height are not available, the lesser man must stand. Social position being equal, age decides seniority."

Many of the ancient rules made clear the relative positions of the castes down to the most trivial detail. For instance, the stick which a Brahman used to brush his teeth had to be twelve inches long. A man from the warrior caste was "instructed to use a stick eleven inches long. The two lower castes were told to use sticks of ten and nine inches.

Those in the higher castes, particularly the Brahmans, enjoyed many privileges under the old social system. If a low-caste person were for some reason to attack a Brahman, the person would be sentenced to death. But if a Brahman were to attack a low-caste person, the Brahman would only be reprimanded for polluting himself by touching an inferior being.

It was the duty of all other castes to support the Brahmans, to give them money, food, and shelter if needed. If a man gave a Brahman a house, some of the codes said, the donor would be blessed with a palace in heaven. If he gave a Brahman a red cow, he would after death receive safe and swift passage across a terrifying river that the dead encountered on the way to the next world.

The Brahman in turn was instructed to be thrifty, kind, satisfied, and generous. He was never to get angry or tell lies, never to sing or dance, never to use an umbrella or wear sandals because this would make him too comfortable, and never to eat any kind of meat or kill any living thing.

Over the centuries, the four major castes were divided into thousands of subcastes. These subcastes were then divided into clans. The exact subcaste and clan to which a family belonged determined the specific occupation of the men in the family and the exact god or goddess which the family worshipped.

For example, two men who belonged to the fourth caste, that of the laborers and workers, were in separate subcastes if the work they did differed. A carpenter and a blacksmith would not be in the same subcaste. Two men in the same subcaste might be in different clans if their families worshipped different gods. To complicate matters further, in some cases two families in different subcastes might regard themselves as particularly close if they happened to worship the same god.

Just as each of the major castes had regulations governing behavior, so each of the subcastes had its own exact rules. These covered every phase of life. For instance, the value and kind of gift one subcaste member should give to a member of another subcaste at various ceremonies was often specified. To give too much or too little was equally bad and could upset village relationships.

Within the subcaste system, some groups enjoyed a higher status than others. Just as a Brahman could not meet a member of a worker caste socially, so a member of a worker caste would not want to socialize with another worker of a lower subcaste.

The result of all this was an incredibly complex social system governed by an elaborate set of rules. It was an absolutely rigid system because no man could ever change the subcaste into which he had been born.

Outside the caste system entirely was still another group —the Untouchables. These were people whose work was sweeping streets, picking up refuse, treating animal hides, disposing of dead animals. Such work was thought to make them unclean.

Strict rules governed the behavior of the Untouchables and their relations with other groups. According to these rules, most of which are no longer strictly observed, Untouchables were not to come into any contact with caste members. Their touch or shadow was considered to be defiling or polluting.

In some regions, Untouchables had to wear tinkling bells around their necks to warn people of their coming. Before entering the gates of one city, Untouchables had to ring a gong hung at the entrance and so signal their approach.

If an Untouchable were fixing a fence in a narrow lane, he had to post signs of his presence at both entrances to the lane. Sweepers in some cities could not appear outside their homes without a broom. The broom immediately told who they were. Untouchables could be admitted to the courtyard of a high caste family. But they could under no circumstances step on the veranda. This would put them on an equal footing with a caste member.

Similarly, Untouchables had to step aside as caste members passed. Everything was so arranged that an Untouchable would always be in an inferior position, always reminded of his status.

Certain Untouchables were also "unlookables." It was forbidden for them to show their faces in daylight or for Brahmans to look upon them. In some parts of India an Untouchable might be punished if his shadow fell across the body of a Brahman. In order to lessen the chance of such an occurrence, several cities passed strict laws that forbade an Untouchable to enter the central part of town after the middle of the afternoon. By that time his shadow was long and in danger of falling on a Brahman.

To make sure that Untouchables did not forget their lowly status, they were forbidden to build houses of stone or wood. They had to limit their dwellings to mud and straw. They were not allowed to own land, wear good clothes, or even try to obtain the kinds of work considered clean.

The complex set of rules governing Untouchables and castes developed over the centuries. Thus Indian society became divided into thousands of water-tight compartments, each containing one subcaste or group having little contact with the rest of society. Within each compartment all men were equal, but there was little equality in the society at large.

Caste Today

The strength of the caste system and the prejudice against Untouchables have both been declining steadily since the start of the 1900s. It is now forbidden by law to discriminate against an Untouchable. Children of Untouchables now sit next to Brahman children in school. Caste Hindus have married Untouchables. There are many poor Brahmans and some wealthy Untouchables.

The growth of democratic ideas and the lifelong efforts of such men as Gandhi and Nehru have led to the gradual weakening of caste and untouchability. Many Indians regard these as systems which may once have helped society maintain some order. Now, however, they are regarded as outdated and evil. The old caste system might have worked in a rural setting. But most observers believe that it is out of place in a society striving to industrialize. For caste hampers . . . freedom and mobility, so necessary for industrial growth.

Nevertheless, ideas which were believed for centuries and which were so important do not die easily. In the villages many caste customs and restrictions, even if not as faithfully observed as before, are still practiced. For instance, the homes of the members of each caste are usually found together in one section. A low-caste man or an Untouchable would not think of moving to the Brahman area of his village, nor would a Brahman move out of his own quarter. The well in each area used to be for the exclusive use of that caste. In practice this remains generally true, although signs may proclaim that anyone may use the well.

Members of upper castes usually bathe thoroughly at the day's end, not only to remove dirt but sometimes to remove pollution picked up from contact with lower castes. In the cities, however, crowded conditions and other aspects of urban life have reduced the strength of caste customs.

In some villages each caste has its separate council house, with another council house for affairs which concern the entire village. A stranger is always welcome at the council house of his caste. But he is not normally allowed to enter the council house of a higher caste, nor would he attempt to do so.

In Moslem Pakistan and Buddhist Ceylon, a caste system as strict as that in most of Hindu India never developed. Instead, an equally complicated system of relationships based on jobs formed the basis of village society. In Hindu India the caste into which a boy was to be born decided his future occupation. In Moslem Pakistan and Buddhist Ceylon, occupations were traditionally handed down from father to son. The result was similar across the subcontinent.

In each village there were families who were always the barbers, carpenters, pottery makers, blacksmiths, tailors, and other nonfarmers. Each of these workers supplied his goods or services to a number of families. These relationships lasted for generations. In return, the families served gave the workers money, grain, clothing, and other needed items. On holidays and special occasions, both families and workers might receive something extra. This system of mutual service was widespread.

In this way, every worker in the village knew exactly what his obligations were—and to whom—and more or less what he could earn. In the insecure world of the subcontinent, this system offered great security. By giving everyone an exact place in the village scheme of things, the system did away with competition. Since workers did not have to compete, they could cooperate.

The system put heavy pressure upon any young man who refused to follow the family vocation. If the son persisted in wanting to be a blacksmith when his family occupation was carpentry, he might even have to leave the village. He was a threat to established relationships.

Moslem and Buddhist men were not free to choose their occupations any more than Hindus were free to choose their caste. This was not a matter of tyranny, but of survival. Suppose those who were expected to follow the carpenter's trade refused to do so. Then how would farm implements be fixed? Even if just one man refused to follow the hereditary occupation, the entire structure of the village economy could be endangered.

A village might find itself without some essential worker, perhaps because the man in that occupation had no sons. Then it would send a delegation to other villages in the district to recruit someone who could be spared. For example, a blacksmith in another village might have two sons, but his village had enough work for only one. Then the second son could be invited to go to another village. Perhaps that other village might try to make the offer more attractive. It could promise the man a house or, if he were unmarried, a bride.

Whatever the problem, there was an old rule to solve it. But in time these rules impeded progress, because they gave only old answers to new difficulties.

The Family

Over the centuries the systems of caste and hereditary occupations helped the villages develop a highly complex, yet stable and orderly society. At the same time, the individual family in India, Pakistan, and Ceylon also developed a complicated set of rules. These governed the relationships in the *joint family*—all the people living in one house or courtyard.

Ramiah, a boy of eighteen, lives in the Indian town of Hyderabad. His father owns a clothing store, has a good income and a house of ten large rooms. Twelve people live in the house—Ramiah, his parents, his married brother with his wife and three children, his two sisters, a widowed aunt, and a widowed grandmother. Such a household, known as a joint family, is common in the subcontinent. When Ramiah himself marries he will be expected to bring his bride to live in the house of his father. He would not move into an apartment of his own unless there were no room in his father's house.

Kamala is a village girl from a poor family. The house in which she lives consists of only two small rooms and a courtyard. But it is shared by herself, her parents, a married brother, his wife and two-year-old son, and an old uncle. When Kamala marries she will go to the household of her husband's father to live. Only in very rare instances do newly married village couples establish a household of their own.

Separate households are set up, however, when sons have many children of their own and need more living space. Sometimes a particularly serious family quarrel leaves no alternative except to break up the family home.

The joint family offers security to the individual. All income is pooled, all food shared. Every person in the joint family is sure that, no matter how hard the times, he always has a roof over his head and a share of the available food. No household, particularly in the villages, would refuse to accept an additional relative in its courtyard. Nor would any son refuse to care for needy parents in their old age, no matter how little he had or how large his own family was.

Today the joint family system has another advantage. It enables young married men to work in the cities while their families are cared for in their father's household. Many men live and work in the cities for years, saving their money, before sending for their families.

The system has some disadvantages. Any family would feel disgraced if one of its members were actually homeless. So it offers him shelter but it won't necessarily encourage him to strike out on his own. Many young men, knowing that their basic needs will be met, are not eager to look for work. Another disadvantage is that when so many people live in close quarters, there is no privacy.

The head of the joint family is almost always the oldest man in the household. His word is law, his position unchallenged. He spends most of his day talking over family affairs with his sons, discussing and supervising farm or business activities, and receiving visitors on his veranda or in the courtyard. This pattern most often occurs in the villages and only if the household head does not have to work in the fields. But even in the cities he makes the final decision on any important family matter, and his advice is sought on all problems.

The head of the household demands and gets the greatest respect from his family. His sons may be well educated, prosperous, and living in the city; he may be illiterate and living in a village. Yet they will bow low and touch his feet as a sign of respect and honor. When an Indian says hello or good-by to his father, he holds his palms together so that the tips of the fingers are at the level of the forehead. This is a sign of the special respect due a parent. In an ordinary Indian greeting, the fingertips are at the level of the chin.

In many villages the head of the household is held in such respect or fear that the younger wives of his sons dare not speak to someone else in his presence. Nor would they even dare address him directly unless he first talks to them. This does not mean that the head of the household is regarded as a tyrant. Rather, his years are believed to have given him the wisdom and experience to make the right decisions.

The oldest woman in the courtyard has a similar position of authority. She is usually the wife of the head of the household. If his wife is dead, then the wife of his eldest son takes over. She has complete charge of all the household work—cooking, cleaning, washing, caring for the children. She may not do much of the work herself, but she closely supervises the work of the younger women, making sure that the household runs in an orderly fashion.

The wives of her sons are expected to obey her and to master all the details of running the household. They prepare for the day when they themselves will assume a position of responsibility. She is frequently critical of their performance. They may complain to their husbands, but there is no remedy except to move to another courtyard.

Among the most orthodox families, a man is scolded by his mother if she sees him talk to his wife during the day. The wife herself is scolded for neglecting her duties or for laziness. Young wives have little status in a village household until they give birth to a son. Only then are they really regarded as members of the family.

A modern Indian mother-in-law is usually not a tyrant. She is really interested in the welfare of the entire family group. Moreover, in the cities, mothers-in-law do not often have the authority they do in the villages, even though they are still given great respect by their sons' wives.

As more young men and women of the subcontinent become better educated and move closer to the modern world, they reject some of the traditional family relationships. Sons, for instance, are insisting that they be allowed to set up their own households when they marry. Wives are demanding that they—not their mothers-in-law—make the decisions about their own family life.

At the same time, many of the traditional rules of family behavior are still observed, especially in the villages. For instance, most village women, and many in the cities as well, always walk on the left side of their husbands. The left is considered inferior to the right, symbolizing the supposedly inferior position of the women. (In some areas, however, the women walk on the right.) The women also walk several paces behind their husbands as a mark of respect.

In the villages, when a husband and wife walk together, it is the woman who carries the bundles on her head and the baby on her hip. The husband may carry nothing at all. For the husband to carry the bundles or the baby when he is with his wife would be contrary to custom. It would also lower his status and social standing. The other men would laugh at him for being dominated by a woman.

In most villages and many cities, a woman does not normally join her husband and his guest in talk. Sometimes, when a male guest is in the courtyard, the woman stands half hidden in the doorway of an interior room. She may even keep herself completely out of sight as long as the guest remains. When the guest is offered tea, the wife prepares it, but it is usually served by her husband. In many regions, custom forbids a wife to serve any male except her husband or members of her family group.

The most extreme form of separation of women from all men except those of their own household occurs in orthodox Moslem families in Pakistan. This seclusion of women is known as *purdah*, which means *curtain*. The women who observe strict purdah go into the street only rarely. Before they go out, they must ask permission of their husbands. When they appear outside their homes, they are completely covered by a white or black tent-like cloth known as a *burqa*. A veil completely covers their face.

Some Moslem men regard it as a sign of their own high status and wealth if their wives observe purdah. It means that the man is rich enough to have servants go out into the streets and do all the things his wife would otherwise have to do. Among strict purdah-observing families, women cannot have jobs, go to college, or have any social contacts except with women of other purdah-observing families. At home a woman does not wear the burqa. However, if an unrelated male comes to visit her husband or any other member of her family, she instantly disappears.

Many in Pakistan do not observe purdah. Among poor families, the women must work in the fields and appear in the streets as part of their normal activities. They could not do their work in a burqa or avoid the presence of men. Nor is purdah observed by the families of many government officials, businessmen, and others who want Pakistan to move more quickly into the modern world. Many girls now go to the universities. They, too, do not observe purdah.

Like many of the other old traditions, purdah is slowly
giving way to the demands of modern times.

PAKISTAN'S P.O.W. WIVES [2]

The neighbors of Mrs. Nasim Khan ignore her now. Mrs.
Freda Shah's friends are reluctant to phone. Mrs. Naheed
Badar stays home each night, yearning to see a motion pic-
ture in the city.

"I haven't seen a film in more than a year," said Mrs.
Badar, a young, sad-eyed mother of two children. "I must
remain indoors and wear dark clothes. I mustn't go out,
especially in the evening. I am a widow whose husband is
alive."

Mrs. Badar and her two friends are wives of Pakistani
prisoners of war. Their husbands are among the 93,000
Pakistanis who have been held in fifty Indian camps since
the strife in Bangladesh in December 1971. Although the release of the prisoners is a deeply emotional political issue in
Pakistan, the activist wives of the P.O.W.s are, ironically,
the object of scorn and dismay in the rigid social atmosphere
of this Moslem nation. [In the latter half of 1973, a gradual
return of the prisoners began.—Ed.]

"It's Unheard Of"

"It's difficult for a woman to survive alone in our society
and people can't accept the fact of a woman leaving her
home to work or speak publicly," said Mrs. Shah, the con-
vent-educated wife of a Pakistani army engineer. "Here the
only place for a woman is to be hidden. When we demon-
strate, when we talk on television, it's unheard of. I still feel
guilty about it."

Although the Western concept of women's liberation is
remote, the wives of many of the Pakistani prisoners have

[2] From article by Bernard Weinraub, correspondent. New York *Times*.
p 44. Jl. 17, '73. © 1973 by The New York Times Company. Reprinted by
permission.

taken a hesitant, but unmistakable, step toward advancement. The steps have been taken against relentless social pressures.

Lead Demonstrations

"Our society is very inflexible and a woman simply can't be alone," said Mrs. Shah, sitting in the living room of her father's home near downtown Rawalpindi. "People have a narrow outlook. Even close friends stop calling because you're without a husband. A woman without a husband is nothing."

In such urban centers as Rawalpindi, Karachi and Lahore, the wives of prisoners have been virtually forced to drop their silent roles and accept responsibilities that are rare for middle-class Pakistani women: visiting shops alone, conducting business transactions in stores and banks, arranging trips to relatives, driving cars, making basic decisions about schools, phoning doctors, lawyers, insurance agents.

Beyond this, a group of the women have made the unusual gesture of turning into public figures, leading demonstrations urging the release of the prisoners. The P.O.W.s are hostages in the fierce dispute involving two other stranded groups on the subcontinent: the 150,000 to 175,000 Bengalis stranded in Pakistan and seeking to go to Bangladesh, as well as the 600,000 to 900,000 Biharis, or non-Bengali Moslems, in Bangladesh.

"A woman's place was always around her children and her home and pleasing her husband," said Mrs. Khan, the wife of a lieutenant colonel in the Army's legal branch and the general secretary of the National Council for the Repatriation of Pakistani Prisoners of War. "Outside interests were discouraged. We rarely went out. My husband was quite religious. Then, suddenly, he was captured and I felt everything was lost.

Experiencing Hardship

"Our society is so conservative that it's difficult to step outside the house alone," said Mrs. Khan, a firm, self-assured mother of four children. She was sitting in her small brick house, wearing the traditional shalwar, or trousers, kurta, the long shirt, and shoes with shimmering beads.

"Some of the neighbors look at me and turn the other way," she said. "When you get into the car alone, people don't like it. It's not done. They talk about it. And, of course, I'm lucky because I have some education. I can accept it. What about the women in the villages, the women with no education and no money and a husband who's a prisoner? These women are going through extraordinary hardship."

Within the villages the wives of prisoners receive only sporadic government payments—lower-grade enlisted men earn about $15 a month—and live with mothers-in-law.

"We visit the villages and the women are crying and praying to God," Mrs. Khan said. "They never get along with their mothers-in-law and there's always bickering about money, about the children, about what to do."

"The wives are frightened and treated miserably and there's nowhere to go for them," Mrs. Khan said. "The women say that there is no life without a husband and they might as well be dead. And in villages that's how people treat a woman without a husband." ...

Mrs. Khan recalled that two friends, an Italian couple, invited her and her four children for a weekend away from Rawalpindi. "My brother said, 'No, I don't want you to go with foreigners, it is wrong for a woman with children to go away without a husband,' " she said quietly. "I didn't go."

The women receive an average of one letter a month from their husbands in P.O.W. camps in India. At this point, the wives of the prisoners are uncertain about the impact of their struggle for an affirmative role in Pakistani society—and are, perhaps, confused about what their role will be when the prisoners are released.

"I know, once my husband returns, my status will be the same and I will return to the house," Mrs. Khan said. "But it is a question of the future. Perhaps we have changed things for younger women. We have appeared on television. We have spoken out. We have demonstrated and shown independence. Perhaps now things will change for our daughters."

About two miles away, Mrs. Shah sat in her living room, sipping a cup of tea and watching her five-year-old son, Mahir, play with a ball nearby. "We will never be the same," she said quietly. "I know I don't have the courage to change my life but I know, too, that something has changed permanently. Young girls now seem to want such a different life. We all had arranged marriages and now you hear of girls who want to choose their own partners. It's so different now."

Mrs. Shah smiled and said: "I have three daughters and I know they'll be different than me. But I'll still want them to have arranged marriages. That's the way things are. I couldn't get used to any other way."

INDIFFERENT INDIA [3]

The other day, a twenty-four-year-old Indian salesman was struck by a truck on the busy highway south of New Delhi. For six hours, he slowly bled to death in the blazing sun while hundreds streamed by in cars, on bicycles and on foot. Nobody gave him water, nobody came near him, nobody reported his plight to the police post less than half a mile away. After the salesman died, a reporter asked some curious onlookers why none had called for help. The answer was: "We don't want to be involved with the authorities."

Six hundred miles east of New Delhi is Bihar, a state rich in untapped underground water but poor in its people. Bihar became famous through its suffering in two successive years of pitiless drought. The rains came this year [1968] and the crop is adequate. I went to Bihar after the famine to see what changes the disaster had wrought. In the villages between Patna and Gaya, one of the hardest-hit districts,

[3] From article by Bernard D. Nossiter, correspondent. *New Republic.* 158: 19-21. Je. 22, '68. Reprinted by permission of The New Republic © 1968 Harrison-Blaine of New Jersey, Inc.

earthen bunds or embankments had been built everywhere to trap the precious rainwater. But in nearly every village, these works were falling apart, riddled with holes, crumbling. They had been built during the famine by villagers paid with relief money. Now that the emergency was over, the relief funds had stopped and nobody was looking after the bunds. "Why can't you maintain these embankments with your own voluntary labor," I asked. Again the answers were simple. "We are too divided here to work together," or "Why should I labor to help someone else."

These two unremarkable incidents illustrate a disturbing and little discussed trait that runs all through Indian life. There is here an overwhelming indifference of man toward man, an astonishing absence of any social sense that extends beyond the family. It is not accurate to say that India is a jungle in which every man's hand is raised against his fellow. Conscious and deliberate cruelty occurs only sometimes. Caste villagers have maimed or tortured erring untouchables. The army burns suspect tribal villages in the troubled northeast and reported killing two hundred rebelling Naga tribesmen May 27 [1968]. But this is not the common mode. The prevailing condition here is unconcern, a lack of imaginative feeling for others.

It is displayed in dozens of daily events. I have driven cars through the difficult traffic of Paris, Rome, Tel Aviv, Teheran, Karachi and Colombo. But nothing matches the destructive anarchy of Delhi or Bombay. Trucks, buses, autos, motor scooters, bicycles and pedestrians relentlessly pursue their own path, heedless of other people. They wander across lanes, cut out into the center of streets, make left turns from the right and run through stop lights with a joyless, solipsistic abandon. This is not, as sometimes suggested, a phallic impulse of a suppressed people liberated in a powerful machine. The same blind indifference marks the driver of a big lorry and the rider of a spindly bicycle.

The tone is set by authority. India's independent government was encouraged by its former British masters to erect impressive new buildings for its administration. Bulky and awkward stone and plaster piles have sprung up in the heart of the capital. But their intended effect is diminished by the army of middle- and lower-level officials who work inside. They casually flip cigarette stubs, tea-time crumbs and chewed pan leaves onto the floors of their new offices. Hallways are speckled with the red betel juice spat out by passersby. Pools of urine stain some corners. Courtyards and walks are littered with trash, tossed aside by inmates and public alike. I recall a conversation with one high official that was interrupted by his sudden need to expectorate—from the nearest open window to the ground below.

A newly arrived villager who squats by the city roadside to defecate or urinate is simply following the conventions of his community. But within Indian cities themselves, there is little effort to instruct people in the sanitary requirements of large agglomerations. Indeed, it is dubious if the effort would work without a far-reaching change in the attitudes of one Indian toward another. Meanwhile, much of the population, particularly in hot weather, suffers from dysentery and all the other debilitating diseases carried by flies swarming over the compost and garbage heaps.

"Ah, but that's Asia," the old hands say. It is not, of course, as China and Japan demonstrated long ago. Closer to home, neither Ceylon nor Pakistan suffers from anything like the same lack of social sensibility. Its absence in India affects such routine matters as mailing a letter with ten cents worth of stamps. Unless the sender sees the postage canceled with his own eyes, he cannot be sure that a clerk will not sponge off the stamps for himself. Any bulky letter or package stands a good chance of being rifled unless a registration certificate, documentary evidence of its transmission, is purchased.

There is something absurd in the pop cult image of India now at large in the West. Nehru, Gandhi, Ravi Shankar, the Maharishi Mahesh have created a vague picture of a gentle India, removed from worldly concerns with a meaningful if imprecise spiritual message for affluent materialists. What Gunnar Myrdal calls the "diplomatic literature" of American officials and academics has left this image as unsullied as the rose in Nehru's coat. The plain fact is that social undiscipline is a taboo subject. Polite and committed Westerners are not supposed to discuss it; a few Indians do, but evasion and euphemism are the preferred style. This is unfortunate, for the lack of social sense, of fellow feeling, plays a significant part in India's failure to modernize its economy.

Some Indian writers . . . have attempted to explore the sources of Indian insensitivity. Their findings are tentative but they suggest that the roots are buried deep in the nation's cultural history. For perhaps four thousand years, the region has been inhabited by conqueror and conquered, exploiter and exploited. The former have maintained order in part by creating a multilayered social structure with racist undertones.

The caste system itself appears to have begun with the Aryans who poured across the Gangetic plains from the northwest. The invaders kept subject the earlier inhabitants of the Indus Valley by imposing the strict divisions of caste. The structure appears to have brutalized both those on top and bottom. The caste system reserves functions for different groups and enforces its hold by an elaborate network of marriage, eating and other taboos that strip dignity from men. . . . Those at the bottom tend either to fawn on those at the top or labor under them in sullen and mute resentment.

Most important, perhaps, is caste's creation of a class of unpersons, those of no caste, the untouchables. Today, nearly every Indian village contains its separate and miserable cluster of hovels for those outside the caste order. Thus most Indians grow up alongside a human group seen as defiled, as objects. In an attempt to soften this relationship, Gandhi coined a new term for untouchables, *Harijans* or "Children of God." However, the word itself reflects the patronizing of a caste figure. The Indian constitution, of course, has outlawed untouchability. But its writ in this sensitive sector does not run as far as the traffic policeman's. The institution remains unshaken in most villages and its dehumanizing consequences spread throughout Indian life.

In a curious way, Hindu religion reinforces this structure. Perhaps unique among the world's sacred books, the Vedas [a group of writings on which Hinduism is based] do not urge the equality of man and man. The more humanistic ethics of Buddha may have tempered this spirit at one time, but eventually, Buddhism was absorbed in India and found a more comfortable home elsewhere in the East.

The lines between conqueror and conquered were redrawn by successive invaders. Moguls were followed by the British, and all left behind a legacy of superior and inferior. Independence was supposed to shatter all this. It has not. The newly liberated civil service, for example, hungered for all the race-proud outer trappings of the Raj. Today, outside any government office, clusters of "peons" wait to open doors for their masters and lowly chaprassis [official servants] scramble after cold drinks and tea. Indian writers have frequently noted the extraordinary rudeness with which many officials treat citizens, a caricature of the British manner. Less commonly observed is the discrimination in favor of Europeans. Petty clerks will frequently serve "whites" out of turn, even against their will, and despite a long line of waiting Indians who got there first.

The sophisticated official at the top is usually beyond this crude racism, or almost so. But if his parents advertised for a bride when he first entered government service, the chances are that they specified what caste should apply and suggested their preference for a "fair-skinned" mate. It is uncertain how far removed the most worldly Indian is from racial feelings. Not long ago, an important official with an international reputation was talking privately of the rebellious and illiterate tribes in northeast India. He spoke contemptuously of the "savages" and suggested that negotiating with them would diminish the dignity of India. . . .

Apart from class, caste and color, there are other forces that make Indians insensitive to their fellows. One of the most powerful may be the institution of the joint family. The obligations to relatives are intense and pervasive. In the villages, uncles, cousins, sisters and brothers generally live under a single roof. This may strengthen family feeling but it may also breed hostility or indifference to any larger group. This inward turning afflicts those most in need of mutual support, the untouchables. In a Harijan settlement in Bihar, I was reluctantly told of an old widow who had starved to death despite the distribution of free food in a caste village two miles away. Too weak to go for the grain ration herself, she asked a neighbor boy for help. The Harijans were evasive about what had happened, but apparently the boy had used the ration for his own family. There was some shame in the community about telling this to an outsider. But no one seriously blamed the youth.

These observations are not recorded out of malice or wish to shock. I believe that there is an intimate relationship between India's disappointing economic performance and the life style of the Indian people. The diplomatic literature conventionally attributes India's static expansion to a wrong mix of economic policies—neglect of agriculture, infatuation with heavy industry, too much or too little regulation of enterprise and the like. But I suspect that economics is too narrow a discipline to explain what has happened. A climate of extreme egoism is ill-suited for economic development.

India's able economists draw up elaborate development plans; they go largely unheeded. Indeed, the planners have taken a holiday for the past two years and their absence has been barely noted. Inevitably, Indian administration is casual and capricious. A forest of regulations to govern industrial growth has sprung up. Its chief fruit are the licenses that determine the life and death of a firm. Predictably, licenses are granted or denied in the same undisciplined fashion in which Indian people behave. Favoritism and bribery, not the plan's requirements, decide who gets what. In agriculture, success for a farmer today depends on his ability to obtain credit, fertilizer, high-yielding seeds and assured water. All are in short supply. Again, the allocation of these crucial inputs has much more to do with a strong farmer's influence over the local credit cooperative and the Block Development Officer than any paper plan.

The Indian government and its American AID [Agency for International Development] patron have quietly worked out a new strategy that implicitly recognizes and tries to exploit the lack of social cohesion here. Under the euphemistic label of "Intensive Agriculture," a deliberate effort is being made to channel the scarce resources to the biggest farms. Only lip service is now paid to the great unfinished tasks of land reform, insuring the security of the great mass of tenant farmers on the land they till and distributing land to the landless. It is conceivable that the strategy will work—this year's bumper harvest is cited as evidence—in the sense that substantial gains in total output will finally be registered. But the widening gap between the spoilsmen—kulaks [farmers with relatively large holdings of land] at the top and the scores of millions at the bottom is unlikely to foster social cohesion.

The remarkably successful agricultural revolutions in Japan and Formosa were based on a different principle, great increases in yields by small farmers with an intense self-interest in cultivating their own plots. To ignore this lesson and consciously encourage a favored minority could in time light the fuse that will explode this fragmented society.

The diplomatic literature is developing a new line of argument to counter this fear. It contends that the divisive forces themselves work against disorder. In this view, caste is a social cement, insuring stability: every man in his place and the places are fixed. But this appears to be based on a false historical analogy with feudalism. Stability in the medieval world—and there is increasing evidence that it was far less stable than the conventional historical view—rested

on a two-way flow. Manor lords and villeins had duties toward each other as well as rights. No such relationship exists
here. The aggressive Jat farmer of Haryana [a state in northern India] has only the most shadowy of obligations toward
the tenants or landless laborers who work his land.

Perhaps nowhere is the lack of social cohesion better
demonstrated than in the selfish agricultural marketing system now in vogue. In the midst of the record harvest, famine
is reported in several districts of Assam and Orissa [in eastern
India]. The rich yields of the Punjab and western Uttar
Pradesh are unlikely to reach these people; each state or
group of states husbands its own supply.

It is a commonplace that modern industrial society re-
quires a measure of cooperation and loyalty. The absence of
these qualities has more than an incidental effect on the neglect of machinery and the shoddy output in many Indian
plants. The planners have set ambitious goals for manufac-
tured exports, goals that must be reached if India is to earn
her way in the world. But businessmen, responsive only to
narrow conceptions of interest, adulterate everything from
milk to toothbrushes to automobiles; their workers, imbued
with the same antisocial sense, are not likely to improve the
dismal product of their masters. India's prospects of selling
more abroad are hampered as much by this undisciplined
performance as by any tariff barriers in the outside world.
But again, a powerful and privileged few will survive and
survive handsomely. They know how to weave in and out
of the web of controls to protect themselves from foreign
and domestic competitors. The great complex of high-rise
luxury apartments springing up around Bombay's Malabar
Hill and financed by tax-evading business money is testimony to the ability of a few to live comfortably amidst
social anarchy.

In discussions of India's needs and problems, the diplomatic literature has centered on such questions as an adequately motivated program of birth control, the prospects
of the Congress party, the private financing of fertilizer

plants and the requisite quantum of foreign aid to achieve something called "takeoff." I submit that equally relevant and much more resistant to change are the indifference, callousness and selfishness that have become imbedded in Indian society.

INDIA'S ENDLESS TROUBLES [4]
Reprinted from *U.S. News & World Report.*

India as a nation is not poor. Its $50-billion-a-year national economy is one of the ten largest in the world.

India's people as individuals, however, are desperately poor. Their great numbers—about . . . [570] million—turn a big economy into one of the world's smallest per capita incomes, less than $80 a year.

The result is that India and its people, despite strenuous development efforts and massive foreign aid, are trapped in an orbit where poverty, outweighing economic growth, threatens to be self-generating.

The great mass of Indians are rarely able to save or acquire enough capital, even $100 or $200, to lift themselves and their families out of impoverishment. Nationally, this means there are not enough wages, profits and savings to tax, or money to borrow, for development that could break the poverty chains.

The tragedy is that India should by no means be doomed to endure its shackles. It has great natural resources and human skills.

But . . . more and more analysts have warned that, unless there are quick, drastic changes in the economy, the poverty cycle will get worse.

Straws in the Wind

There are worrisome signs that this is already happening. Some examples:

Industrial output expanded only 5 percent in 1970—half of the planned target. In the first six months of 1971, factory production inched ahead only 1 percent.

[4] From article in *U.S. News & World Report.* 71:86-9. N. 8, '71.

Unemployment is growing rapidly. Urban joblessness, now estimated at 16 million or more, is expected to swell to 28 million by 1974, and to more than 50 million by 1979.

Food-grain harvests have been rising, and reached a record 107.8 million tons in 1970. But agricultural authorities warn that the easy gains are in the past; there is almost no chance of achieving planned increases by 1980.

These are the hard facts of India's enigma, the numbers and percentages economists and planners must work with. More relevant to the future—especially in preserving the world's largest democratic government—is how these numbers and percentages shape lives and welfare of individuals.

To understand what a poverty cycle like India's means in individual terms, visit four representative Indians: a struggling Calcutta street vendor, a Rajasthan farmer who still does not own a pair of shoes despite doubled harvests, a New Delhi industrialist who believes in more workers and fewer machines, and a family-planning worker to whom a measure of progress is having a place to sit down and talk with the villagers she counsels.

Sidewalk Vendor

In his tiny clothing stall made of packing crates and rough planks on a teeming Calcutta sidewalk, Gopal Chandra Saha talks about how close to impossible it is even for a hard-working Indian to break away from bare existence and "take off" toward self-sustaining growth. Gopal's own take-off target is 1,000 Indian rupees—about $135.

"With that, I could expand my business enough to save 15 rupees—about $2—a month," he explains. "Then I could buy merchandise directly and make more profit. But now I can't save anything. I don't see any chance of ever getting as much as 1,000 rupees."

Gopal, only twenty-one, has been selling cotton shirts and underwear on Calcutta's streets since 1962. Even setting up a street stall was a big financial gambit. It meant raising about $8 for deposits with the half-dozen wholesalers he deals with. This took all the family savings, plus hard scrimping for many months.

Shirts at Gopal's stall cost 50 cents; men's shorts are 7 to 20 cents. His commission is less than 1.5 cents on each sale. But his reputation as an established sidewalk merchant is good, and his prices are right for his slum neighborhood, so business is fairly brisk. Turnover averages about $150 a month; Gopal's earnings about $15.

On this he supports himself, his wife, parents and two younger brothers. Usually his wife stays with her parents, partly because Gopal's one-room home is so crowded and partly because it reduces chances of her getting pregnant.

"I want very much to have sons, but we do not dare," he says. "There is no room for them, no money."

Though Gopal lives off the consumer market, his own skimpy purchases show one reason why India's economy is so precarious.

The rent he pays for a slum room with no electricity, water or toilet is about $2.50 a month. A government-subsidized "wheat ration," including grain, sugar and cooking oil, costs another $2. The family would prefer rice, but wheat is cheaper. About $4 monthly goes for fresh vegetables. A piece of fish is a rare treat.

One thing has improved for Gopal. Before 1967, he recalls, he could work only in the afternoon. Almost every morning, the police drove street vendors off the sidewalks. The difference is that in 1967 a Communist-run government came to power in Calcutta. The Communists are out of office at the moment, but not out of Gopal's mind.

"I would like to see a Communist government again," he says. "Business for us is much better when they are in power. Maybe I could save something."

Blend of Modern and Ancient Societies

India is at the same time among the richest and poorest, most advanced and most backward nations on earth. There have been dramatic advances, but shortcomings remain.

When India became independent only twenty-four years ago, it was basically a commodity supplier and market for finished goods from Britain. There was next to no industrial base. Now Indian factories turn out complex computers, jet aircraft and nuclear reactors, along with consumer goods ranging literally from autos to zippers.

Thousands of miles of dusty paths have been replaced by hard-topped roads. Powerful tractors pull farm machines across fields once tilled by shuffling bullocks and wooden plows.

India's railways, one of the world's biggest and busiest networks, are making plans for turbojet trains capable of reaching speeds of 180 miles an hour. Indian firms are winning contracts in competition with European and American companies to build power stations and steel mills in other countries.

The trouble is that signs of India's progress shrink almost beyond recognition when measured against the country's statistical numbers and its needs.

Some 200 million people—nearly equal to the entire US population—live on less than 15 cents a day. Over half of the 2.8 million government workers earn less than $15 a month and are rated lucky to have regular jobs. The rural poor, perhaps 40 million of the most deprived of India's people, are mired so deep in poverty that some economists say they should not be included in development planning; direct subsistence handouts are cheaper.

Labor specialists say inflation and industrial stagnation have reduced real earnings of the bottom 10 percent of India's workers by one fifth in the last decade. A $65 million crash program to create half a million rural jobs in the coming year is lagging badly.

In the past decade, India's literacy rate has jumped from 16 to 30 percent. However, the total number of illiterates climbed from 298 million to 386 million.

Farmer

The drama of India's "green revolution" that has made the country almost self-sufficient in grain, along with nagging doubts about its future, is seen on the twenty sun-baked acres that Ganga Ram farms on Rajasthan's arid plains, twenty miles west of Jaipur.

Ganga Ram, barely literate, knows nothing about national agricultural projections. However, his experiences shape them. His ninety-foot-deep well and two pumps, costing more than $2,150—an outlay equal to the average yearly income of 27 Indian farmers—irrigate only eight of the farm's twenty acres. This has doubled average harvests, but the well goes dry in some years. Even in wet years, it can be pumped only five hours a day.

This means that Ganga Ram cannot use chemical fertilizers, which burn up crops when constant, adequate irrigation is not available.

Ganga Ram uses some high-yield "miracle" seeds, especially wheat, mainspring of the green revolution. Like most Indian farmers, he experiments cautiously, sowing the new seeds only an acre or two at a time.

"We cannot take a chance on something going wrong on all the land at the same time," he explains.

The question—on Ganga Ram's farm, and all across India's croplands—is whether grain harvests will continue expanding without greatly enlarged irrigation systems and wider use of chemical fertilizers. "Miracle" seeds require both for extended effectiveness.

Ganga Ram has little access to the technical advice and the credits that help make American farms so productive. No one from the national or state ministries of agriculture has ever visited his farm. His soil has never been scientifically tested.

Ganga Ram did borrow 7,000 rupees—about $950—from a government bank for the two pumps. But the terms are stiff. The entire farm, worth at least ten times the amount of the loan, had to be pledged as security, and the interest rate is 7.5 percent a year. But a village moneylender, the only credit source for most rural Indians, would charge at least double that interest rate.

Some economists predict higher farm incomes will boost consumer-goods demand, spreading the green revolution through the entire economy. In the wheat-rich Punjab region this is happening. Farmers are buying tractors, radios, and electric fans, and building better houses.

But the twenty people living as a communal family on Ganga Ram's farm—typical of rural India, though more prosperous than most—do not own a bicycle, clock or radio because "there is no money for such things."

They buy some clothing, but Ganga Ram owns no shoes. Other purchases include school supplies for the children and some jewelry—more for investment than for adornment.

Race to Stay Even

Less than a decade ago, a bridge of ships loaded with food from overseas kept India from starving. This year the country is feeding itself with very little belt-tightening. Wheat output has doubled. Over all, output of food grains climbed 6.5 percent in the past year. The number of tractors in use soared 100 percent in five years. Most farmers eagerly adopted better seeds, confounding some experts' predictions that this would not happen in a traditional society.

But the green revolution still is only a marginal success. Grain self-sufficiency at present—and even at projected levels —means for India's masses a bare minimum of calories; a diet severely lacking in protein and other nutrients. There has been no breakthrough in rice, the single most important food grain and the basic staple in areas of densest population. Expanding individual farm irrigation by drilling single wells may be reaching its limit. Needed are canal-irrigation systems that take massive capital outlays not now available.

On planners' charts, India will grow 113 million tons of grain next year, 129 million tons by 1975. But some authorities are highly skeptical. A recent World Bank report said flatly there is "no possibility" of meeting those targets.

Industrialist

A growing number of people believe there have been significant blunders in efforts to break India's chains of poverty. One who thinks this way is Manmohan Singh, a Sikh industrialist in New Delhi.

"The politicians have never given the economy a chance to let itself go," he contends. "Their values are those of the villages, where the votes are. They cannot conceive of a big push to a big economy. We need production so badly that you do not have to be a good executive to make a profit; you just have to produce."

Manmohan Singh's ideas about a big economy and how individuals and nations achieve one began taking shape in 1948, when he was a refrigeration-engineering trainee at the Frick Company in Waynesboro, Pennsylvania.

Recalls Manmohan Singh:

"The first morning there I showed up wearing a suit. They put me to work on a cement mixer in the foundry. I thought, 'This is no place for me,' but I had to keep face, so I buckled into whatever job they gave me."

In India, he says, there is too much importance placed on "face," too little on buckling in.

"We have too many people who only want to sit at a desk and administer things," he says. "Advertise for a secretary who can type and you get a reply, 'Dear Sir: I understand you have an opening for an executive.'"

After working his way up to head of Frick's research department—a job that began with pushing wheelbarrow loads of junk from a laboratory basement—Manmohan Singh returned to India to represent the company.

Today he is head of Frick India, manufacturers of heavy air-conditioning equipment and a subsidiary of the Frick Company of the U.S. The company has a factory near New

Delhi which employs 650 people. The subsidiary's Indian shareholders have put about $300,000 into the company, and last year [1970] they received a 12 percent dividend.

Manmohan Singh is not sure that India offers as much individual opportunity as it did a quarter century ago. But he is completely convinced that there would be better opportunities for Indians in general if economic advisers took a different tack.

"They fail to use our biggest economic asset—cheap labor," he insists. "They want everything the most modern, heavily capitalized. India cannot afford that."

At the Frick assembly building is an illustration of his idea: the tube-bending department, where one man fits a piece of pipe into a crude, homemade bending device while four others pull on the opposite end with a rope.

They take the place of a $70,000 hydraulic bending machine I was going to buy, and that any government factory would have [he explains]. Each of the men earns four rupees—about 55 cents—a day. They bend all the pipe we need. In India, you must look for every opportunity to produce the same quality goods with more labor, less capital and machinery. The planners will not see this simple fact.

By Indian standards, Manmohan Singh is very well off, with two cars, a suburban home set in a spacious garden, vacation trips for his family. Yet he does not consider himself one of "the rich," and worries that if India does not soon find a solution to its unending poverty, businessmen will face increasing trouble.

"The poor here are more and more aware of the disparity between rich and poor," he says. "They know the rich get richer while they get poorer. The government knows this, too, and blames it all on the businessman. That is good politics but bad policy." ...

Inefficiency at the Top

India's industrial economy has both the capacity and demand to make it a powerhouse nation. Instead, it barely limps along.

Big government-owned steel mills and electrical-machinery factories operate at 40 to 75 percent of capacity in a nation of shortages. Lost production—more than two million tons of steel last year, nearly one third of the national demand—generates other bottlenecks. Makers of steel pipe, auto parts, nails, farm equipment and hardware say that steel shortages hold down their output. Structural-steel shortages have cut new construction in half in some cities.

Steel-mill managers blame frequent strikes, often politically inspired, for the shortages. Workers and some outside analysts say inept management is equally at fault.

Threatened closure of a big West Bengal paper mill, building delays at a Bombay power dam, and brick shortages in Harayana all are laid to lack of railroad cars to haul lumber, cement and coal.

Freight-car builders say their output is down two thirds . . . because government-run railways refuse to buy cars despite break-even prices. Railway officials reply that there are plenty of cars, but they cannot be used efficiently because of strikes, signal-wire thefts, and lawlessness that make train operations dangerous for crews in many areas.

Family Planner

If India never realizes its full potential, the reason simply may be too many Indians, increasing too rapidly. With the biggest population-control program in the world, India also struggles with one of the biggest population growths.

That struggle to close the gap is told by Laxmi Kutty, twenty-three, a family-planning "motivator" in Sirsi, a Northwest India village, about fifteen miles south of Jaipur.

"There is some progress," Miss Kutty says. "When I started here three years ago, people sometimes stoned me and pushed me out of the village. Now they at least offer me a place to sit down while I talk."

But Miss Kutty thinks that effective population control is far away. She explains:

Peasant farmers still hold to the theory that if they have more children, there will be more hands to work in the fields. If anything goes wrong, even a stomachache, after a man has a vasectomy or a woman is fitted with an intrauterine device, they blame it on that. We cannot make the usual tests after a vasectomy and, under field conditions, a number are not successful. So some wives get pregnant after the husband's operation and the village labels her a "loose" woman. Then we are set back for months.

In Miss Kutty's district, with more than 38,000 people, there were only 67 vasectomies and 30 IUD insertions last year, well below 1969 totals and 1970 goals.

Miss Kutty talks with about twenty-five women every day. Most days she knows she has not brought even one family to solid acceptance of family planning. She suspects that many other districts meeting or exceeding quotas "do it by operating on over-age people who don't have babies anyway."

Pessimists say that India's population bomb already has exploded; that people already born will overwhelm the most strenuous efforts to defuse it. They may be right. Population now is growing at a rate of 13 million a year—about equal to the entire population of Australia.

A Glimmer of Hope

Even if India achieves the extraordinary feat of cutting its birth rate in half, the population will exceed one billion by the year 2000. Optimists who say that India somehow will control its population growth because it has no other choice hope that the trend will be reversed before that time.

For all the difficulties, every year important numbers of Indians do manage to escape from the poverty cycle. A slowly growing, though financially hard-pressed, middle class testifies to that. But many experts warn that this is not enough to pull the mass of chronically poor along with them. There is noticeable progress, but India's ever-growing needs nullify it.

The challenge, for most Indians, is to lift themselves by their own bootstraps—when they have no shoes.

URBAN SQUALOR [5]

Once Karachi was the cleanest city in the East, with tidy streets. At midday the British drove to beach huts for a swim in the cool Arabian Sea.

"Now we are a city with every conceivable urban problem," said Abbas Hussain Shah, the burly, fast-stepping director general of the Karachi Development Authority. "Lack of water, sewerage, drainage, housing, transportation —name the problem and Karachi has it. We are trying to deal with these things, but it's like climbing a wave that tends to overtake you each time."

The Pakistani government is struggling to lift Karachi, the nation's former capital, out of the urban squalor that keeps at least 200,000 people sleeping on the streets and more than a million living in hovels made of burlap bags and mud. To the government—as well as to local planners —Karachi is an embarrassment.

"What has happened to the city hurts me no end," President Zulfikar Ali Bhutto said recently. "We have to make efforts to improve it, clean it, do something. We've had this wholesale influx of refugees, hordes of them, and now we have a city of slums and disease. We have to do something now."

If Karachi is gripped by intensifying chaos and despair, it is also the most throbbing city in Pakistan. The literacy rate is the nation's highest. More than 80 percent of large-scale business is in Karachi, which provides nearly half the income-tax revenues.

Miles and Miles of Misery

On the negative side, what especially disturbed the government was a recent statement by a Thai health official who was quoted as telling a World Bank meeting that Karachi was rated the dirtiest city in the world, followed by Calcutta.

[5] From "Karachi, a Clean City Once, Is Now a Trough of Urban Squalor," by Bernard Weinraub, correspondent. New York *Times.* p 7. Jl. 14, '73. © 1973 by The New York Times Company. Reprinted by permission.

The official later denied making the comparison, but Pakistanis concede that the city is swollen with packed slums and swept by miles and miles of human misery.

The city is a victim of the violence that accompanied partition of the subcontinent in 1947, when the British left and India's Moslems carved out Pakistan as an Islamic state. A pleasant backwater harbor city of 400,000, Karachi suddenly emerged as the capital. Within three years the population had climbed to a million as Moslems in India fled across the partition line (Hindus fled in the opposite direction). Now there are more than four million squeezed into Karachi, and the population is increasing by 7 percent a year.

"What do you do, how do you cope with this kind of unparalleled growth?" said Mazhar Rafi, administrator of the Karachi Municipal Corporation. "People come here now because Karachi is the business center, Karachi is the place for jobs."

"We are a city that hasn't been able to cope with our problems because the problems are just a bit overwhelming," he said.

In addition to being the industrial and commercial center of Pakistan, Karachi seethes with street life. Zaibunnisa Street and Jinnah Road are crammed with bicycles and donkey carts through the day and into the night, along with crowds of shoppers, children, veiled women, beggars and hawkers. Garish pink and blue bungalows, signs of affluence, cluster beside rows of shacks, lit by candle at night. In narrow steamy bazaars thousands of men have tiny stalls to sell cigarettes, trinkets, food, clothing, watches and seashells.

"Karachi is the center and will always be the center of Pakistan, said Abdhar Khan, a watch seller whose father came from the Punjab to Karachi in 1947.

Sitting at his stand in a sweltering bazaar near busy Frere Street, Mr. Khan said in Urdu: "There's nowhere else to go in Pakistan. If you want to make money, if you want a life, you go to Karachi."

Because the capital was shifted in 1960 from Karachi to Islamabad—partly the result of Karachi's vulnerability to India—the city has suffered deeply from mismanagement, improper planning and odd overlapping.

At least half a dozen government bodies—the navy, the Karachi Port Trust, the municipal authority, the army, the railways, the Public Works Department—administer separate areas and jealously guard their domains.

"How can you kill mosquitoes in one area if two streets away a different agency doesn't want to bother?" asked Mr. Rafi, a trim, cheerful man. "What's the good of killing mosquitoes if that happens." . . .

Karachi is scheduled to undergo the most crucial administrative change in years: There will be elections for an autonomous metropolitan government, with a mayor, to run the city.

At the same time the federal government, aided by a United Nations technical-assistance team, is in the midst of a "master plan" project for the city at a cost of $12 million. It will be designed to encompass a sprawling region of four thousand square miles; urban Karachi covers about 350 square miles now.

"This is a classic example of a primate city," said Mr. Shah, the development director, as he drove his jeep on a recent afternoon when heavy rains flooded slum areas. "We have the best of industry, most of the vehicles, the majority of telephones. People naturally have to come here, and things break down."

"Now we have the added element that people are demanding action, demanding change for the first time," he continued. "We had thirteen years of rigid military rule when people were scared of bureaucrats. Now they're scared of nothing and making demands that Karachi has got to change."

Mr. Shah's development budget has climbed from $150 million in 1972-1973 to $255 million in 1973-1974. "We are trying to deal with the most basic things," he explained as he and a visitor passed through the stricken, reeking slum of Lyari, near the port. "It's a question of developing plots and putting sewerage and water in so people can at least start out with some sanitation."

FOR INDIA:
THE KEY TO DEVELOPMENT [6]

India has a wealth of folklore, folk art, and traditional forms of communication, including puppet plays and dance. It also has surprisingly well-developed channels of modern mass communications. There are seventy radio broadcasting stations in the country and 12.8 million licensed receiving sets, and since most of the latter are played at top volume, the radio audience must be at least 100 million. The mass medium par excellence in terms of appeal and popularity is the cinema. India is now the world's number-one producer of feature films and weekly cinema attendance is estimated at 30 million. There is scarcely a small town without at least one movie house and sprawling bamboo and thatch movie palaces can be found at many of the more important rural crossroads. To these is now being added television.

The government plans to put approximately $400 million into the development of a national television system in the Fifth Plan, with terrestrial transmitters in every state capital and a geostationary satellite for bouncing broadcasts directly to selected village clusters. The government believes that TV can be a powerful instrument of national integration and can promote agricultural development, better health and nutrition, famliy planning and the like.

Unfortunately, as a series of seminars sponsored by the Ministry of Information and Broadcasting have frankly revealed, existing or planned effective use of this rather formidable communications infrastructure is crippled by a serious "software gap."

[6] From article in *Development Forum,* published by the Center for Economic and Social Information of the United Nations (Geneva). 1:5. Ag.-S. '73.

There are few development-oriented programmes in any of the media and those that exist tend to be either dull and didactic or pitched at a level only the better educated can understand. Little has been done to combine entertainment and instruction. The Hindi and other Indian language feature films that are such box-office smash hits set the pace for entertainment, but their message, insofar as they carry one, is antidevelopmental.

According to an analysis presented by Mr. Feroze Rangoonwalla of *Film* magazine at a recent panel meeting on satellite television, the hero of the typical Hindi film is a likeable, passive young man. The heroine is a likeable, passive (and very good-looking) young woman. The villain is the active type—the only person who practices "scientific method," according to Mr. Rangoonwalla—and for about the first hour and a half of the film he does very well for himself. "Scientific method" loses out in the long run, however, for in the last reel the hero always triumphs through some completely gratuitous stroke of luck or fortune. It is all very good as wish-fulfillment fantasy, but wish-fulfillment fantasies are about the last thing India needs at this stage of its development.

An experimental video tape recently produced with UNDP [UN Development Program] assistance points the way to a more effective use of modern media. It is edited from live-action sequences filmed on half-inch video-tape portapacks in the field.

Produced in a drought-affected locale in Rajasthan with the cooperation of the Ministry of Agriculture, the tape was made in an unusual three-part process. First, there is a free-wheeling discussion among a group of farmers. The farmers had heard there were government loans available for deepening their wells, but they seemed confused about how to obtain these loans. Separately, local government officials gave their side of the story. Finally, the two groups were brought together and shown the already-taped sequences while their reactions and subsequent discussions were again taped. The effect is startling. In the final scene, as each side sees things from the other's point of view, a new and lively rapport develops. Viewing the three sequences in order in the final edited version, one sees two-way communication in action.

UNICEF [United Nations International Children's Emergency Fund], too, is seriously applying itself to assisting in the solution of India's communications problems. There is a large and complicated chart hanging on the wall of the UNICEF Audio-Visual Studio in New Delhi showing just what communications support needs to be built into each part of the early-childhood-services effort from now through 1979. It covers everything from newspaper campaigns to prerecorded tapes for hospital waiting rooms. UNICEF supports this communications work as best it can all along the line. The chart features two previously neglected areas at the extremes of the communications spectrum where UNICEF plans a special push: mass media for children, and "village pump" communications to achieve better child care.

Television prototypes will spearhead the mass media push, simply because the field is wide open and because now is the time to make sure that children get a fair shake of the dice when TV does materialize on a national scale. A fair shake means giving the child something he really needs in terms of his development in a particular environment. This work will be handled by a Children's Media Lab which is being hatched under the wing of the Ministry of Education with UNICEF support. Stories, characters and situations which work, will be translated into other media, too, such as comics, radio plays, games, slide sets and posters. One favourite character is a talking horse who plays a sitar. He could be used in a lot of different situations and media if children take to him.

At the "village pump" end of the spectrum, . . . UNICEF is . . . sponsoring a study in five rural areas to develop the simplest possible messages and audio-visual aids package for parents. This package is aimed at getting across the four or five key concepts parents need to know to give their young children a better chance of survival and development in an environment rife with hostile microorganisms and malnutrition.

UNICEF has engaged an Indian consultant to develop a kit, compact enough to be packed into an attaché case which will enable field workers to shoot, edit, process and exhibit their own filmstrips, even in the absence of a darkroom. UNICEF feels that what is lost in professional expertise will be more than gained through personal identification and involvement.

It is not just the villagers who can benefit from media designed to motivate and encourage. For the government of Maharashtra state, UNICEF is producing a film to motivate medical graduates to take up rural practice. More precisely, all medical graduates in Maharashtra must put in two years' rural service or forfeit a large bond. This film is designed to encourage a more positive approach toward their rural practice and to make these future doctors consider more carefully before simply dismissing this period as another hurdle to overcome before hanging out their name plates in towns. The film will be shown at medical colleges at the beginning of the rural internships. Incidentally, more and more Indian states besides Maharashtra are requiring this internship of doctors before they can take up full practice.

What can a film do to make young doctors more willing, or at least less apprehensive, about serving in rural primary health centres? They have just finished six years of intensive schooling. Many feel they'll rot in a rural atmosphere. Those trained as specialists are afraid of missing chances of professional advancement. Young women medical graduates complain they'll be hopeless old maids by the time they get back to city life.

The film brings these apprehensions into the open and puts them into proper perspective, alongside tangible satisfactions of a young rural centre doctor who is doing a good job. In the beginning, things go badly for him, only two patients a day show up at his clinic because his predecessor, a semiqualified "old doc," didn't inspire confidence. His quarters are shabby with leaking roofs and city newspapers arrive three days late. There is nobody with his educational background to talk to and the worst fears of the medical graduates are confirmed.

But then the young doctor gets out of his office and begins to participate in rural life. His attitude changes to "as long as I'm here, I might as well do a good job." His clinic fills up and he realizes the people need and respect him. For this young man who has always been a student, this is a new and good experience. The two years will pass more quickly than he had imagined—perhaps too quickly.

This rural doctor film is only one component of the broad effort UNICEF is now launching to strengthen the communications aspects of their child-centred programmes throughout India, but not an insignificant one. In addition to its direct purpose, this film may indirectly serve to encourage the scores of young Indian film-makers to stop imitating European nouvelle-vague pictures of yesteryear and explore human interest angles of development in their own areas.

III. THE INDIAN ECONOMY

EDITOR'S INTRODUCTION

A great deal has been written about the Indian economy in the last ten years. The articles tend to fall into two categories: those which portray the economy as being hopelessly inadequate and predict catastrophe, and those which concentrate on the progress already made and predict a bright future. Perhaps the most realistic view lies somewhere between these extremes.

India has indeed made striking advances in the agricultural, industrial, and technological fields. An array of statistics indicates that fundamental change is taking place in many parts of the country. Yet, it is also true that the results of this progress are often swallowed by the increases in population or else affect only the small progressive minority, leaving the mass of people unaffected and untouched.

The articles in this section address themselves to the positive and negative factors of the Indian economy. The first article, which presents both dark and bright sides, asks whether India can make it. Not unexpectedly, no clear-cut answer can be given. But an informed opinion can be drawn from this examination of major difficulties as well as more encouraging developments of the past ten years.

The next selection offers a detailed view and review of the economy. The author, Phillips Talbot, a man with long experience in India and Asia, concludes that the progress made in the first generation after independence holds promise for the future. One of the important positive factors is the so-called green revolution, which is discussed in the third article of this section. As the article indicates, however, the green revolution is not an unmixed blessing, for it has brought new problems.

Despite the green revolution and the vastly increased grain harvests since the mid-1960s, hunger is a fact of daily life in India, as described with painful clarity in this section's fourth article. While abundant crops may bring about surplus in one state, transportation and other problems sometimes make it difficult to ship that surplus food to deficit areas. The result is hunger.

The last article offers a brief insight into the economic planning mechanism of the Indian government. Though India has one of the world's more sophisticated planning bodies, the commission's knowledge and experience is not always able to cope with the complexities of the economy.

CAN INDIA MAKE IT? [1]

"I would like a simple yes or no answer. No long lecture. Is India going to make it or not?" The question came from a very prominent Washington economist who fixed me with a beady eye . . . the day after I had returned from five years in India. Five years is too long for a simple answer, so I said, "India is one sixth of the human race. Is the human race going to make it?"

There are . . . [more than 570] million people in India—more than in all of Latin America and Africa combined. They are about one sixth of the . . . [more than 3.7] billion people on earth, and they are one third of the people in countries the UN classifies as less developed. Their ethnic and cultural variety is greater than that of all the nations of Europe. Their economic skills range from hunting with a bow and arrow to the export of machine tools.

[1] From article by Robert R. R. Brooks, Orin Sage professor of economics, Williams College. *Saturday Review.* 52:12-16. Ag. 9, '69. Copyright 1969 by Saturday Review Co. First appeared in *Saturday Review,* August 9, 1969. Used with permission.

India was put together in 1947, for the first time in its five-thousand-year history. Nine provinces and six hundred autonomous princely states were fused . . . in the crucible of partition.

India is still a nation, and as far ahead as anyone can see —say twenty-five years—it will remain a federal union with substantial central power. No armed force capable of challenging the army, air force, and navy; no separate foreign policy; no competing external revenue collection; no displacement of central control over interstate transport and communication—none of these is likely to occur in the foreseeable future.

For a country with more than three hundred languages, fifteen major scripts, skin colors ranging from blue black to ivory white, six major social classes, hundreds of castes, thousands of subcastes, eleven major religions, nine major political parties, four major trade union movements, sixty-seven universities, and about two million college students— this degree of national unity after twenty-two years as one nation is a remarkable phenomenon.

But Indian politics is decentralizing. The process has been going on for seven or eight years. It became apparent after the death of Nehru in 1964, and striking after the losses of the Congress party in the elections of 1967.

In a very real sense this is not a retrogression, but a recognition. The centrifugal forces inherent in the heterogeneous mass of India were concealed by the unity required for the expulsion of the British, the discipline and idealism of the Congress party, and the charismatic personality of Jawaharlal Nehru. Following his death, and as the euphoria of independence receded and the Congress leaders grew plumper and older, the local and parochial dissidences— which had been there all the time—were revealed. Indian unity was ahead of its time.

The United States has approximately 200 million people spread over fifty states. The federal power is relatively great. India has more than 500 million people in only seventeen states. The federal power is relatively small. One of these Indian states—if it were a separate country—would be the eighth largest in the world. Others are nearly as large. India is, in political fact, a group of countries with separate linguistic, military, ethnic, and dynastic histories. By any normal historical standard, its federal unity is a miracle—or, at least, premature. The center of political gravity, when it comes to rest, is bound to be in the states.

Despite the strong powers accorded to the central government by the constitution, the substantial financial resources of the national government, and the powerful military and police forces at its command, most of the big barons of New Delhi are the political bosses of the states.

And yet, India will not dissolve. Why not?

The principal answer is: Hindu culture—that inexhaustible complex of religion, mythology, literature, esthetics, tradition, class, caste, struggle, survival, repression, aspiration, good sense and nonsense, absorption and rejection, violence and patience that binds the subcontinent into a nonorganic but cellular unity.

The second answer is the civil administration. Trained to maintain order and collect taxes, it has been called upon for difficult tasks in socioeconomic development: community programs, agricultural improvements, family planning, industrial growth, export promotion. The civil servants are posted from state to state, from state to center, and center to state. Their shortcomings are many and sad, but the best are superb and the worst still maintain order, obey commands, keep records, and carry on the indispensable minimal functions of law.

The third answer is the constitution that prescribes state, central, and joint powers enforced by an independent judiciary, permitting the central government to take over local rule if state authority collapses and providing presidential powers which could—as a last resort—supersede those of the parliament if representative government became deadlocked.

The fourth answer is that Indian policy is profoundly influenced by an educated elite—widely distributed in all the principal cities; sharing the English language; wanting national independence, but needing worldwide associations and assistance; dedicated to development, but alternating between hope and despair.

And finally, India is laced together by such mundane but practical ties as hard-surfaced roads, railroads, airlines, telegraph, telephones, postal system, canals, electric power lines, and an industrial capacity to produce most of the equipment that enables these services to work—fairly well.

Of all these things that work—fairly well—the grandest by far is the Indian-made Mercedes engine and chassis. Roaring down mountain curves from Ladakh to Kashmir, grinding through the sands of Rajasthan, scuttling as a bus or groaning as a truck, lumbering, carrying soldiers to the front, taking villagers to market, picking up fish in Trivandrum, or moving oil in Gujarat—it is everywhere, a tyrant of the roads and a testament to the ubiquity of change. The fact that this engine and chassis—with an endless variety of carriers mounted upon them—are made in India suggests that Indian industrial development is remarkably advanced.

India has limitless quantities of high-quality iron ore, ample low-quality coal, and an immense hydroelectric potential, partially harnessed. Its petroleum resources are being developed in Gujarat, and exploration continues. It has phosphate rock in Rajasthan, and iron pyrites for sulphur.

It has a rapidly growing chemical industry. It has been producing textiles for a century. It makes its own telephone equipment. And, surprisingly, it makes all sizes of machine tools—of sufficient quality and quantity for export to "advanced" countries.

But there are problems: One is a multiplicity of economic controls that causes delays, encourages monopolies, discourages efficiency and initiative, and invites the corruption of the regulators by the regulated. Another is the scarcity of managerial skills and the thinness of external economies—indispensable to large-scale enterprises. Still another is the politicizing of the labor movements to a degree that contributes more to disorder, violence, and destruction than it does to the welfare of workers and the productivity of industry. A fourth is bottlenecks in the supplying of certain raw materials and many small parts—especially those which have to run the gauntlet of exchange controls and scarce foreign exchange.

But the greatest problem of all is the lack of a mass market. People are abundant, but their incomes are too low to exert a demand-pull on the expansion of industry.

Population appears to be growing at more than 2.5 percent a year. This means an annual addition of 13 million people. The Indian government is making a greater effort than any other nation to reduce its rate of population growth. The objective is to bring it down to 1.5 percent in the next ten years.

In absolute terms, the numbers of loops inserted, condoms distributed, and vasectomies performed under government auspices seem very large. But, relative to the total population, they are pathetically small. Even if this effort were multiplied manifold—as it will be—the rate of growth may rise for several years before it begins to fall. There are two reasons for this. First, the death rate is still high compared to developed countries, and will almost certainly continue to drop, barring mass starvation. Secondly, India's efforts during the past twenty years to eliminate epidemic and endemic diseases (especially malaria) have been successful in reducing infant and child mortality. Millions of children who would otherwise have died fifteen years ago are now approaching childbearing years. This sharp shift in age composition will tend to raise the crude birth rate, simply because there are more childbearers per thousand of population now than there were ten years ago.

With a falling death rate and a high birth rate, the *growth* rate could rise to 3 percent before it begins to turn

downward. This would be very discouraging to family planners and to those who wish them well. Were it not for the
impressive birth control efforts, the increase in the growth
rate would be even larger.

For the next ten years, the principal hope of avoiding
mass starvation in India is an annual increase in domestic
food output sufficient to keep ahead of population growth
and to reduce the country's dependence upon uncertain
food imports. What are the hopes?

The key to India's future—and indeed to that of two
thirds of the human species—is rising productivity in agriculture. All political dogmas, party slogans, planning strate-
gies, and models of economic growth shrivel to irrelevance
in the face of this fact.

There can be no industrialization without a surplus of
food from farmers to feed industrial workers. There can be
no urbanization without a surplus of food in the countryside
to feed the city. There is little prospect of absorbing the unemployed and underemployed except on the farms. In a
nation 80 percent rural, there can be no mass market for
industry unless rising agricultural productivity gives farmers higher incomes with which to buy the products of industry.

And although increased rural incomes would not guarantee political stability in this age of rising expectations and
seething frustrations, they are a prerequisite to any possibility of extending the degree of economic cooperation and
interdependence fundamental to economic progress. The
signs are clear that India's leaders have recognized this and
have, for several years, given agriculture superpriority.

The problems, however, are enormous. First is the political problem. The No. 1 rule in economic planning is not
to scatter scarce resources but to concentrate them at the
points of greatest productivity. This runs exactly counter to
the egalitarian conviction that each should receive according
to his need—that even the least productive, and therefore the
poorest, areas should get central funds and attention. More-

over, in any country as loosely integrated as India, each state, district, block, and village *panchayat* [village council] is in a strong position to demand its share. But scatteration is the path to the wilderness.

The government showed courage in facing up to this dilemma by shifting its emphasis from the universalized Community Development Program to the Intensive Agricultural District Program (IADP). It compromised by putting at least one intensive program in each state. But in so doing, it tried to pick the most likely district.

The IADP is an effort to pull together all the inputs required for high productivity: good land, water, good seeds, fertilizers, pesticides, credit, price incentives, drying facilities, storage, and transport—among others. The amount of planning, organization, incentive, cooperation, patience, and determination required is prodigious. But it is India's hope, and the results, after several years of preparation and effort, sustain the hope. It now seems likely that between the crop years of 1967-1968 and 1968-1969, including a good and a poor monsoon season, food grain output increased by about 6 percent—well ahead of population increase.

Although all of the inputs responsible for this agricultural growth are important, the most important, after water, is chemical fertilization. Indian food output per acre is among the lowest in the world. Most of the arable land has been farmed for two or three thousand years and has been progressively depleted. The biological cycle for restoring soil fertility is inadequate for high yields, and is bled outward by the use of cow manure as a fuel instead of as a soil nutrient. Only chemical fertilizers (soluble nitrogen, phosphate, potassium, and trace minerals), plus some organic material to maintain the friability of the soil, can raise India's food output fast enough to feed its people.

India's consumption of fertilizer has increased sixfold, from 200,000 tons of nitrogen in 1962 to 1.2 million in 1968. Since it does not pay to use heavy doses of fertilizer unless all the other inputs are present—especially water and the new seeds which accept a large fertilizer application—the increased fertilizer consumption is a good index of progress in other aspects of intensive agriculture. Supply, demand, and distribution of fertilizer have been keeping a reasonably even pace with one another. The time is well past when critics questioned the Indian farmers' acceptance of chemicals. And India now has in production or construction about 2 million tons of nitrogen capacity. The goal is 5 million tons by 1975.

If the nitrogen goal is reached and is balanced with phosphate and potassium production or imports, India can be self-sufficient in food by 1975 in terms of providing the projected population for that year with a more nearly adequate caloric intake and protein content. But this is a very large "if." Among the elements to be considered are the following:

1. A continuation and improvement of the present policy of inviting Western business to collaborate with Indian public and private firms in a rapid expansion of fertilizer production

2. The development of private systems of fertilizer distribution and sales promotion in competition with the government-sponsored cooperatives

3. Expansion of the IADP to additional districts, with especial emphasis on reliable water supplies

4. Patience and vision on the part of Western enterprise in seeing the opportunity, despite maddening delays and frustrations, presented by the vast Indian market for agricultural inputs

5. Development of indigenous extraction and refining of phosphate and sulphur

6. Continued expansion and improvement of the research and extension services of the universities and government agencies to cope with the multitude of problems—virus, bacteria, fungus, soil deficiency of trace nutrients, and blowdown—which inevitably follow the introduction of new seeds into alien soil

7. Pricing, taxation, and land-tenure policies that provide security for investment in land and incentives to cover the risks of new methods

8. Enough foreign exchange to buy the fertilizer and its ingredients until India can produce most of them itself

Despite a 1968 gain of 9 percent in exports over 1967, India had a foreign-exchange gap of $1.4 billion last year [1968]. India has suffered considerable inflation, especially as a result of food shortages caused by the terrible droughts of 1965-1967, and the 1965 war with Pakistan. But the inflation has been far less than that of most developing countries, and, relatively speaking, India has been fiscally temperate, if not conservative.

The Indian government courageously devalued rupees from 4.75 to 7.50 to the dollar in 1966, but the world demand for India's basic exports is so inelastic that the devaluation only slowly assisted in promoting exports. The rupee is probably still overvalued by perhaps 20 to 25 percent, but an additional devaluation would be very risky politically and would accomplish little in export promotion.

India has the most rigorous system of import controls of luxury goods and consumer durables of any non-Communist country. Although this creates a black market in smuggled consumer goods and invites corruption of the exchange and customs controllers, the scarcity of imported cars and other durables is visual testimony to the general effectiveness of the controls. On the other hand, India has greatly relaxed its import controls over raw materials, spare parts, and components for high-priority industrial development.

In addition to the millions of tons of P.L. 480 [Public Law 480—Food for Peace program] food grains sent by the United States in 1968 for rupee repayment, India had to spend $250 million for food imports to avert hunger. The fertilizer, phosphate, and petroleum imports were all directed primarily at expanding food production. In the cold figures of the foreign exchange gap the tragic need for food is icy clear. When and if India, with its own resources, can nourish its soil and feed its people the gap will disappear. But unless the gap is filled for the next years with foreign economic assistance, there is little hope that India can make it.

During the past twenty years, the United States has loaned or granted about $9 billion to India including about $4.5 billion in P.L. 480 food grains from our formerly embarrassing food surplus. India is the largest gross beneficiary of our aid, but has received by far the smallest per capita assistance. The largest annual amount loaned by the United States to India was $435 million, or about 87 cents a head—three years ago. Since then, our help has sharply declined to a probable $250 million in fiscal 1968-1969.

Non-US loans to India, principally from the United Kingdom, West Germany, Japan, the World Bank, and Eastern bloc countries, have been on shorter maturity and tougher terms than ours. Unless these creditors accede to an extended moratorium on the $500 million now annually owed, there is no prospect of closing the gap and little political possibility that our Congress will increase foreign-aid funds which are vitiated, in part, by repayments to others. If a moratorium is negotiated, the gap will be reduced to $900 million. Of this, the US share should be about $650 million.

Why "should" we do anything? India's "teeming millions" will not pose a threat to us in the foreseeable future. Should we pour in more money to salvage what we've already sent? It would be cheaper to write it off. We don't need India's natural resources. Does India offer attractive markets and opportunities for investment? Yes, in the long run, but for the next twenty years it will be just as profitable and a lot more pleasant to deal with Canada and Western Europe. Even with substantial United States Government guarantees, private US investment will, for a long time, provide only a small portion of the funds needed to make India self-sufficient.

Do we need a powerful counterpoise to China in South Asia? In old-fashioned diplomatic terms, perhaps yes. The departure of the British from the periphery of the Indian Ocean from Capetown to Singapore left a vacuum that India ought to fill. But the Chinese have problems of their own. They are not likely to climb the Himalayas to acquire India's food deficits. They will make border trouble—indeed they are busily at it in Nepal, in Assam, and in Burma. But India is in a far better position to cope with border troubles now than it was in 1962.

India will not turn Communist for a long time, if ever. Both the Soviet and Chinese Communist parties in India are utterly irrelevant to the problems of the Indian masses. They are brutally capable—with their combinations of unemployed intellectuals and hired plug uglies—of obstructing parliamentary government, destroying property, and violently impeding production, especially in West Bengal. But they are a long way from being able to cope with India's army and central government. So, again, why should we be concerned about the country's future?

India's people compose nearly one half of the population in less-developed countries outside of the Communist bloc. It is a sizable sample of the future. At present relative rates of population growth, the less-developed countries will soon have five sixths and then seven eighths of total world population. What kind of company do we want as we ride our tiny pellet through space? Do we want to be surrounded by miserable masses consumed by hunger, misery, envy, hatred, violence, and disintegrated into the primary biological units from which we began our long ascent ten thousand years ago? Or would we like to make a relatively small financial bet on the hope that man can someday achieve the dignity for which we used to think he was destined?

Five years ago we were providing economic and military assistance to the less-developed countries at the rate of about $4.5 billion a year. This year, at a much higher GNP, we will offer less than half as much. If we and our like-minded friends were to loan India $900 million in the coming year, and offer the same average per capita rate of assistance to all the rest of the underdeveloped countries, including China, the total bill would be less than $4 billion, excluding debt repayment. The US share of this should not be more than $3 billion—with $650 million for India.

Will India make it? Will the human race make it? It depends.

THE ECONOMIC STRUGGLE [2]

During the 1971 national elections and the 1972 state elections, Prime Minister Indira Gandhi's New Congress party adopted the slogan, *gharibi hatao!* (banish poverty!) As a campaign cry, the motto was heady and generally successful; the reality, however, is harder. India *is* a poor country.

It is also a country with ambitious economic goals. When India gained independence from Britain in the wake of World War II, Mrs. Gandhi's father, Prime Minister Jawaharlal Nehru, pointed to the mammoth tasks ahead and told his compatriots that "this generation is sentenced to hard labor." Few Indians today would deny that the same sentence must be passed on Mrs. Gandhi's generation and probably on its children as well if India's economy is to grow as they desire it to.

At the time of independence the Indian economy was faltering. Apart from endemic poverty the new national leadership had to wrestle with immense immediate difficulties. Agricultural production was stagnant. India already had a limited industrial base, but many of its factories and much of its national transport had been depleted by overuse in the war effort and by inability to get replacements. World trade terms put India at a disadvantage.

[2] From *Understanding India*, pamphlet by Phillips Talbot, president of the Asia Society. (Headline Series no 214) Foreign Policy Association. '73. p 19-32. Reprinted by permission from Headline Series no 214. Copyright 1973 by the Foreign Policy Association, Inc. 345 E. 46th St. New York 10017.

Worse still, the partitioning of India in 1947 to make room for the new state of Pakistan resulted in devastating economic consequences. The new international frontiers between Pakistan and independent India, which were drawn to reflect harsh political realities, made no sense economically. They separated raw materials from processing centers, factories and farms from their traditional markets, water sources from water users. They also left vast pockets of frightened Hindu and Sikh minorities in Pakistan and Muslim minorities in India. As a result, about 12 million members of these minorities fled across the new borders within twelve weeks after the partitioning of the subcontinent. [Hundreds of thousands of people were killed in rioting that occurred at this time between Hindus and Muslims.—Ed.] Within India, the incoming uprooted millions became the first charge on New Delhi's energies and resources. The task of resettling them in towns and villages posed monumental difficulties and for some time consumed all the vigor that the Indian government and public might otherwise have applied to the many other pressing problems of new nationhood. Moreover, the disentanglement of the assets and liabilities of each side after partition dragged on for years and was never satisfactorily completed.

Early Economic Progress

From so fearsome a start, India made significant economic progress. New large dams and networks of tube wells enabled the country to increase its total irrigated land from about 60 million acres to more than 110 million acres by 1970. Electrification, which the villages had hardly known, reached communities containing nearly 40 percent of the rural population. Transport and financial services were substantially strengthened. Skyscrapers began to punctuate the horizons of Bombay, Calcutta and other cities. Industrial capacity expanded sharply, both in quantity and in the range of products produced; such sophisticated equipment as atomic power plants came on the list of Indian manufactures. Of special significance was the impressive increase in food-grain production that resulted from scientific and technological breakthroughs in the middle 1960s. By the beginning of the 1970s, India reached a point where it needed no imports of food grain. But maintaining self-sufficiency required expanding production to cover population growth and presupposed that the monsoons would continue to be adequate.

During the first generation of independence, India's national income doubled in real terms. (The effects of inflation made rupee gains appear to be much higher, but this must be discounted.) Because of the growing population, the average Indian's real income increased by only 40 percent. By 1969 the Indian gross national product (GNP) per capita was estimated at $95 to $110 per year, depending on the method of calculation. Even though rupees buy more goods and services in Indian villages and towns than their dollar equivalents would suggest to Americans, such a level remained desperately low. What's more, the gains hardly touched the lives of at least one third of the population, especially among landless rural workers and urban slum dwellers. Among other Indians, they translated into new prosperity for a favored few and into more adequate food, better clothes and a few extra amenities for the rest.

To attain these results, the Indian government, starting in 1951, concentrated what resources it could mobilize into intensive national development programs embodied in successive five-year plans. Economic growth has not, however, been the sole objective of these plans. In Mrs. Gandhi's words in 1972, increases in the GNP "must be considered as only one component of a multidimensional transformation of society." She called also for "increased self-reliance, wider diffusion of employment opportunities, reduction in the concentration of economic power—all of which are equally important objectives of economic policy making."

How can a poor country reach such goals? In India the ruling Congress party and the parliament opted in the early

years for what they described as a Socialist pattern of society
—an imprecisely defined concept that acknowledges substantial scope for the private sector but clearly subordinates private interests to overall governmental control and management of the economy's commanding heights. This policy has
opened the way for widening governmental participation in
trade as well as in manufacturing, transport and public utili-
ties. In 1972 the Congress party, reacting to a period of shortages and high prices, recommended that the government take
over most wholesale trade in wheat and rice. It also re-
affirmed its support of restrictions on future private investment in such national "core" industries as steel, fertilizer,
chemical, cement and oil.

The Indian preference for expanding governmental participation in production rather than giving freer rein to the
private sector has both economic and ideological roots. Most
economists and planning officials believe that the private
sector cannot mobilize the resources needed for the forced-
draft development to which the country is committed. In
addition, a pervasive distrust of the Indian private sector
exists among most political parties and their academic advisers and supporters. Political decision-makers suspect that
decisions based on the profit motive serve parochial interests
rather than national needs. At every crisis, therefore, the
tendency has been to increase the public sector's role, even
in areas where management and other problems of govern-
mentally owned and operated enterprises have been more
difficult to deal with than in comparable units of the private
sector. This has not, however, extinguished the private sector, which in permitted areas has itself grown along with the
developing economy.

The government-directed economic development planning process in India has never been an authoritarian pro-
cedure, however. It has regularly included a great deal of
democratic participation, involving the central government,
the state governments, private businesses, petitioners on the
part of political parties, consumers and other special in-

terests. Starting with the first formal national plan in 1951, each new five-year plan has been adopted by the government only after passing many hurdles of public and legislative scrutiny both in the states and at the national level. In this, as in other respects, India has demonstrated that it is an open society.

While this complicated consultation process has often led to compromises among contending interests rather than to maximum efficiency, it has also enabled India to move from an investment effort of $7 billion in the first Five Year Plan period (1951-1956) to $14 billion in the second plan period, $22 billion in the third plan period and about twice as much again in the delayed fourth plan period scheduled to run from 1969 to 1974. In 1972 the planning ministry announced preparation of an even more ambitious fifth Five Year Plan, which would again require double the resources necessary to carry out the previous plan.

Agriculture: Progress, Problems

Until recent years, the bleakest part of the Indian economic spectrum was the agricultural sector. Then suddenly, in the late 1960s, agriculture became more buoyant than industry. The scientific, technological and policy changes that brought such dramatic results have come to be known by the general term, *green revolution.*

"Grow more food" campaigns had been a feature of Indian life since World War II. Under the pressures of necessity, independent India has tried a wide variety of measures to open up new land for farming. Prime Minister Nehru placed great emphasis on major irrigation works, such as the Bhakra-Nangal project in the Punjab with its 740-foot-high dam and its 652 miles of canals designed to irrigate about 5 million acres and thus add some 800,000 tons of wheat production annually. Community development programs and agricultural extension services have been established in all states. To intensify these efforts further, concentrated package-plans of interlocking facilities and services were devised for key districts in each of the states.

The Indian government's efforts to build growth into its agriculture have drawn considerable support from outside sources, including United Nations agencies, the United States Agency for International Development and the Ford and Rockefeller foundations. Yet, during the first two decades of independence, results were disappointing. With great unevenness, depending upon the adequacy of each year's monsoon, the output inched up at an average rate of 2.5 percent, or about enough to keep up with population growth but not get ahead of it. Then came successive crop failures in 1965-1966 and 1966-1967. These threw the whole agricultural program into jeopardy. India had to import millions of tons of food grains and other agricultural products. But for prompt shipments under the American Public Law 480 Food for Peace program, disaster would have been widespread.

That was the critical point at which began, providentially, the revolution in Indian food-grain production. Suddenly science, public policy and responsive farmers came together in a new strategy. A new price policy gave greater economic incentive for increased production. The initial arrivals of high-yielding varieties of wheat from Mexico and of rice from Taiwan and from the International Rice Research Institute in the Philippines had already set off intensive research to explore their potentials under Indian conditions. Agricultural scientists quickly discovered that where assured water supplies, intensive fertilizing and more precise farm methods could be brought together, the "miracle seeds" opened possibilities of increasing output not by 10 to 20 percent—the earlier standards of success—but rather by double or treble the traditional yields.

The ensuing four years belied the old argument that Indian farmers are too conservative to change their ways. Led by geometric increases of output in districts with ample water supplies, national wheat production doubled. Rice came along more slowly, but the increase of one third in the total rice crop was also an unprecedented gain. Corn (maize) followed suit. As a result mainly of these advances in principal food grains, the overall growth rate of Indian agriculture doubled to about 5 percent per year, or about twice the rate of population increase.

Even these achievements, so spectacular as compared to prior performance, have not, of course, solved India's agricultural problems. The Planning Commission continued into the 1970s to warn that optimism should be tempered by the known vagaries of the monsoons, on which would still depend the amplitude of crops in rain-fed growing areas. A sharp setback in 1972 proved the validity of these warnings. Despite substantial buffer stocks saved from previous years, drought conditions left India short of food grains and forced it to make purchases in the international market to feed its people. Moreover, many crops—notably the protein-important pulses [a kind of legume], peanuts and the other oilseeds, and cotton and jute fibers—did not initially share in the major increases. Inflation and administrative tie-ups further delayed the planned spread of irrigation and the production of fertilizers in the early 1970s. Also, the national averages, taken by themselves, disguised extremely uneven performances recorded in the various states, some of which made almost no progress in the initial years of great national increase.

Apart from production problems, the Indian central government and many of the states continue to be confronted with other difficult agricultural issues. As of the early 1970s, reforms to limit the size of landholdings still were proving easier to pledge than to implement, so that declared ceilings often bear little resemblance to the actual family holdings of more prosperous farmers. Entrenched resistance to an agricultural income tax has enabled farm families to avoid taxation on incomes that have often risen above those of heavily taxed upper-middle-class urban residents. For less-favored farmers, difficulties in getting adequate credit have persisted despite strong government support for the cooperative movement and despite efforts to make the banks more responsive to rural needs after their nationalization. Transport, storage and marketing arrangements have come under sharp strains with the sudden multiplication of crop tonnages in favored areas. Rural unemployment and underemployment have not only persisted but, in many areas, worsened.

The green revolution has also raised new and urgent social tensions. Its first benefits accrued primarily to those farmers who owned good land, who had access to assured water supplies, and who could obtain the capital or credit to buy fertilizers in much larger amounts than ever before. They were the ones who could now buy more farm machinery, build new houses, develop new life-styles. Secondary and tertiary activities—machine shops, for example—that supported their affluence were also prospering. But others were left out—the cultivators of monsoon-dependent fields, for example, and the millions of landless laborers. What were to be the benefits to them? The new prosperity from high yields had hardly arrived when rural strikes and demonstrations in some districts accented the dissatisfaction of those who saw no share of it for themselves. Finding ways to deal constructively with this malaise has become an urgent requirement.

When all the problems have been listed, however, the evidence remains that India has begun a major breakthrough in agriculture. The problems that face policy-makers in the 1970s are no longer just those of stagnation; some arise from the consequences of rapid if uneven growth. Agriculture is one area in which India has come into the decade of the 1970s with fresh hope for the future.

Industrial Progress and Problems

In contrast to its recently achieved agricultural vigor, India's industrial development surged through the 1950s and into the mid-1960s, but then experienced a succession of disappointing years. Overall investment in industry grew from $42 billion in 1950 to $100 billion in 1965. The bellwether iron and steel industry, which in 1948 had produced 900,000 tons of finished steel, registered a fivefold gain—an important increase but, even so, disappointing in relation to the heavy investment and high priority assigned to it. The production of industrial machinery and equipment increased, however, by twenty-five times, to an annual volume of $4.3 billion. The output of aluminum, starting at only 3,700 tons in the early 1950s, reached 180,000 tons. Petroleum refining capacity went from 450,000 tons to 20 million tons, mostly using imported crude. Power generation increased sixfold. Thermal turbines, hydroturbines, heavy transformers and nuclear power equipment began to be manufactured. Virtually all equipment needs of India's elaborate railway net and its road transport system also came to be met from domestic factories. The production of drugs and pharmaceuticals rose by about seven times.

Then, in the late 1960s, the country experienced a recession that for a time halted much of the industrial growth. Following the poor crop years of 1965-1967, demand dropped. At about the same time, other problems surfaced: major managerial deficiencies became visible particularly in some of the key public-sector undertakings; labor difficulties grew; power shortages interrupted production; heavy losses were incurred. Executives whose prior experience had been in governmental administration discovered how different the requirements for directing industry could be.

The difficulties that plagued industrial production during that recession have proved to be persistent. When key elements of industrial performance continued poor through the first two years of the fourth plan period (1969-1971), the government launched fresh efforts to break logjams and stimulate production. Both parliament and the industrial community agreed, however, that results seemed very slow in coming.

Almost more troubling than any other feature of the economy has been the spread of unemployment, among educated citizens and in the volatile cities and in the villages where both joblessness and underemployment have been endemic but have taken on graver proportions with the over-all increase in population. With the time at hand to prepare the fifth Five Year Plan, Indian development planners have begun shaping a massive attack on the employment prob-lem. Closely related to the possibility of a much more am-bitious plan than India had previously tried to implement is the question of how quickly the country can restore buoy-ancy to industrial production.

Through the years of independence, India's heavy re-quirements of imports have sparked drives to increase exports as well. Like many other less-developed countries, however, India has so far not been able to keep up with the average overall growth in world exports, which have advanced sharply since World War II mainly because of the dynamic trade performances of more-developed countries. In the two de-cades following 1950, India's exports increased at an average yearly rate of only 2.4 percent to slightly over $2 billion a year.

The record would have been substantially worse but for the rise of new types of exports to offset declines in traditional leading commodities. Textile yarns and manufactures, which amounted to 44 percent of India's exports in 1950, dropped to 25 percent in 1970. During the same two decades, the share of tea declined from 13 percent to less than 9 percent. By contrast, India in the postindependence period became a major exporter of iron ore and of nonferrous ores, particu-larly to Japan but also to Eastern Europe. By 1970 India was also exporting more than $100 million of iron and steel, mainly to Japan and Europe. In addition, it had substantially raised its exports of leather and leather products and of fruits and vegetables. Other commodities sold abroad in larger quantities included coffee, fish and fish preparations, cloth-ing, footwear, scientific instruments, electrical and other machinery, and transport equipment.

In Indian eyes, rising exports are essential to pay for the imports that are vital to the national development. Since in-dependence, India's needs from abroad have included vast amounts of foodstuffs (of which the tonnage donated or sold on concessional terms by the United States is valued at $4.5 billion), raw cotton fertilizers, petroleum products, chemicals, iron and steel (in wider categories and larger amounts than the particular iron and steel products exported in recent years), nonferrous metals, metal manufactures, machinery, electrical equipment, transport and other items. So heavy have been these needs that at no time since independence has Indian foreign trade been in balance.

The Role of Aid

The unbroken string of annual trade deficits would not have been possible, of course, but for foreign investment and very substantial foreign grants and loans that India has received. Because of the dimensions of India's requirements, the international efforts organized to assist India in the 1950s and 1960s proved to be the key program undertaken by richer countries to encourage and support modernization in less-developed nations.

Since 1958 most of the contributing countries have consulted regularly with one another and with Indian government representatives in an Aid-India Consortium for the setting of aid levels. Organized by the International Bank for Reconstruction and Development (World Bank) and with the participation of its affiliate, the International Development Association, the consortium has been a principal forum for the review of Indian development programs. The leading partners in this effort have been the United States, Canada, Japan, the United Kingdom and West Germany. France, Austria, Denmark, Norway, Sweden, Belgium, Italy and the Netherlands have also been among the contributors.

Eastern European nations and the Soviet Union, which have lent India somewhat more than $1 billion, mostly for large public-sector projects, have preferred to supply assistance through direct bilateral arrangements.

The total magnitude of foreign loans and grants to India should not disguise the fact that on a per capita basis, Indians have received among the smallest amounts of aid made available to the world's poorer peoples since World War II. . . . Only a few examples are needed to highlight these differences: Liberia, $31.60; Algeria, $14.30; Ghana, $7.60; Turkey, $5.70; Pakistan, $4.20; India, $2.50.

During the two decades following 1950, United States grants and loans, totaling approximately $9.3 billion, made up the largest single component of foreign assistance to India. Outright grants, given mainly in the early years of the program, came to only $460.3 million of the overall amount. As has already been noted, agricultural commodities shipped to India under Public Law 480 were valued at $4.5 billion. Development loans came to $3.3 billion, most of it spent in the United States for goods and services. Export-Import Bank loans accounted for $526.8 million; the Peace Corps and miscellaneous programs, for another $287.3 million. In addition, United States military assistance to India came to a total of $124.3 million in credits and sales.

It is not easy to set these figures in an appropriate context, but one comparison that comes to mind is the relation between aid and the course of Indian-American trade. During the period in which it received this aid, India shipped nearly $5 billion worth of exports to the United States and imported nearly $12 billion of American goods and services. Thus it would appear that about three quarters of the $9.3 billion American assistance had the effect of financing United States exports.

Self-Help

Important as have been the contributions of foreign assistance, the main cost of Indian development has been borne by India itself. The national and state governments have not only levied steadily more burdensome taxes (except on agricultural incomes) but have also incurred very heavy domestic indebtedness alongside India's external debts. In the 1960s alone, the inflationary effects of extended deficit-financing helped push prices to nearly double their levels at the beginning of that decade.

In 1966 a monetary crisis threatened India at a time when foreign trade deficits were running larger than ever before, when foreign exchange reserves had dropped to dangerously low levels and when plan commitments seemed to have over-stretched the nation's financial capacities. After considering other possible remedies, the government moved reluctant-ly to devalue the rupee from the equivalent of 21 cents to 13 cents. Since that point, reserves have again risen and trade deficits have been reduced.

By the beginning of the 1970s, India found the amounts of foreign aid declining and the schedule of repayments of indebtedness for earlier assistance rising. New financial dif-ficulties arose in 1971 with the Pakistani hostilities in East Bengal that drove millions of refugees over into India and culminated in the Indo-Pakistani war in December of that year. Because of differences over the question of Indian mili-tary involvement in the war, the United States and certain other contributors suspended assistance payments to India. The suspension occurred when India and its creditors were already discussing the possibility of postponing some interest and amortization payments to reduce the immediate fiscal pressures on the country's development program.

To avert such pressures, India is putting more emphasis on the goal of self-reliance in planning its future economic de-velopment. To be sure, few Indians believe that foreign aid could be ended abruptly without devastating consequences to India's development. Many, however, are attracted by the example of China's nondependence on outside assistance. They hope that they too can become less dependent on the nations that, they acknowledge, helped them most during the critical buildup years of the 1950s and 1960s.

The management of a complex economy built on so nar-row a base as India's is a highly complicated task. While *gharibi hatao* (to eliminate poverty) is the nation's ambition, more years of struggle must lie ahead if the gains already achieved are to be carried forward to more sustainable levels. The risks of stagnation and setbacks remain, particularly should there be no substantial reduction in birthrates; or successive years of drought return. Even so, the progress made in the first generation of independence holds promise for the future of the Indian people. Their ability to keep pressing forward will depend on more than technical economic factors, however. Perhaps even more significant may be the viability of the nation's governmental and political institutions.

PUNJAB, BENGAL AND THE GREEN REVOLUTION [3]

Indira Gandhi has changed the political map of the Indian subcontinent, but she has not changed the villagers of Bengal and the Punjab nor the way they grow their food. The emergence of Bangladesh as a separate country has been widely interpreted as the beginning of a three-way power struggle for southern Asia, with the Russians the winners of the first round and the Chinese and the Americans the losers. It can also be seen, perhaps more realistically, as the most dramatic episode thus far in a slide toward social chaos and savage struggles to hold or seize, in both Bengal and the Punjab, resources that have been made even scarcer by the complex forces of overpopulation, cultural uprooting and rapid agricultural change.

The triggering mechanism seems to have been the successful adoption in the past five years of American farm technology in northern India and Pakistan. The newly introduced dwarf, short-stemmed wheat and rice can triple harvests since they can be heavily fertilized with nitrogen without collapsing under the weight of the heads. These new strains have brought both India and Pakistan close to self-sufficiency in food for the first time in thirty years, but because of a lack of social leveling, both between the region of the Punjab and Bengal, and between the rural rich and poor within each region, it has caused a series of political explosions which are only beginning.

[3] From article by Richard Critchfield, correspondent. *Nation*. 214:134-7. Ja. 31, '72. Reprinted by permission.

Chances are that extremely leftish dictatorial governments, not much influenced by either Moscow or Peking, will eventually emerge in Bengal and the Punjab. The Chinese stand to reap gratuitous benefits, gaining recruits for Maoist revolutionary movements from the multitudes of dispossessed peasants, but they will be preoccupied by overwhelming problems at home as their own population nears 1 billion in the 1970s. The Russians are handicapped in poor, agricultural countries because they persist rigidly in trying to transfer their own experience of moving directly into rapid industrialization without first putting food production on a sound basis. Of the three great powers, only the Americans possess the vital agricultural technology.

While the recent focus of attention has been on Bengal, what happens in the Punjab, closer to the real heartland of the subcontinent, will probably be more pivotal. To take each region in turn:

The Punjab is a broad, flat and fertile plain reaching from the headwaters of the Ganges north of Delhi up to the foothills of the Himalayas and the Hindu Kush near Peshawar. Its name means land of the five rivers, for it extends across five rivers that come together to form the Indus, where man, probably migrating from Mesopotamia, created at Harappa and Mohenjo-Daro one of the first river-valley civilizations. In the 1947 partition of India, the Punjab, like Bengal, was about equally divided between India and Pakistan.

Most of today's Punjabis are descended from the Scythian warrior tribes of central Asia who did not enter India until the time of Caesar and did not seize all the Punjab's villages south to Delhi until one hundred years ago. Despite the passage of centuries, they have kept the rough Scythian warrior spirit, glorying unabashedly in strength of arms, the destruction of ther foes and the number of their cattle. Unlike the Bengalis, they never came under the domination of the priests and holy men of the Gangetic plain, who managed elsewhere on the subcontinent to set the whole life-negating tone of Indian intellectual life.

Today the Punjabis are divided about equally into Indians and Pakistanis, and further divided by religion into Sikhs, Moslems and Hindus. Although Punjabis form the bulk of the Indian and Pakistani armies and have now gone to war against each other three times in twenty-four years, they are physically and culturally very different from the rest of the Indians. A strong sense of shared identity persists, as was evident in the favorable treatment captured Pakistani soldiers received from their fellow Punjabis in the Indian army.

Despite its rivers, the Punjab receives only 5 to 15 inches of rainfall a year. The British irrigated this virtual desert with canals which, by the 1930s, served 12.4 million acres. Punjabis were colonized by the British on twenty-five-acre farms and the Punjab became the breadbasket of India. But its population rose 50 percent within a generation and by World War II the region had an average grain surplus of only 5 percent. The Punjab was sinking back toward stagnation and subsistence farming when, along with Bengal, it was the scene of the partition holocaust of 1947, six million Punjabis and Bengalis being uprooted and another million dying in the exchange of populations.

The restoration of the Punjab's agriculture began in the 1950s when the Indian and Pakistani governments both invested heavily in massive hydroelectric projects, introduced rural electrification and subsidized the sinking of hundreds of thousands of tube wells. The truly spectacular transformation, with the new seeds, heavy use of nitrogen fertilizer, tractors, threshing machines and combines giving the Punjab a per acre wheat output nine times higher than that of Kansas, has come only in the last five years, and has somehow escaped general attention.

The decline of Bengali agriculture and disintegration of the Bengali village began, as in Punjab, in the 1940s, but it has never been arrested. The problem has not been too little water but too much. The floodwaters of the Ganges and the Brahmaputra are two-and-a-half times greater than those of the Mississippi and the Missouri; some 60 percent of the region goes under water during the summer monsoon.

In some of Bengal's most densely populated districts, . . . a steady regression in methods of cultivation has been going on now for two generations. No Bengali landholding of less than 1.5 acres can support a pair of bullocks, and the average farm size of 1.7 acres conceals the reality that half the holdings are less than half an acre. Bengal has therefore undergone a steady retreat from oxen-pulled plows to primitive hand hoes, an agricultural revolution in reverse. . . .

The death toll in . . . [the] fourteen-day war [of 1971] is estimated to be between 10,000 and 20,000, including soldiers and civilians, but no one knows how many died in the march of ten million refugees to India or how safe from continued reprisals are the million or so Moslem Biharis and a small number of Punjabis who settled in East Bengal after the 1947 partition. . . .

In both the Eastern and Western halves of Bengal during the past five years there has been a steady growth of movements by dispossessed peasants, who lack bullocks, money, land or hope, to seize land by force. These Naxalite gangs, named after the village where the land-grab movement began, roam about, killing, looting and condemning landlords by "people's courts" on the old Chinese pattern. Until recently, they defined a "landlord" as a peasant with more than 5 acres. Now the standard is down to 3 acres.

The Mukti Bahini, Bangladesh's new army, is commanded by professional officers, but it numbers at most 100,000 men, the bulk of whom are young civilians, and it cannot hope to police the villages where most of the seventy million East Bengalis live. The army is also reportedly infiltrated with Awami League extremists far to the left of the new Bangladesh government, and a wholesale bloodbath and movement to seize land in the countryside, directed especially against the Razakars who collaborated with the West Pakistani government, may be hard to stop. . . .

The obvious danger facing India is that East Bengali Marxists, owing allegiance neither to Moscow nor Peking, will succeed in capturing the leadership of the secessionist battle. From March [1971] until now, there has been an apparently deliberate effort to destroy the ability of the Bengalis to organize, since not only moderate Bengali politicians, intellectuals, officials and other potential leaders have been murdered but even rank-and-file policemen and similarly humble people in the administrative machinery. The blame for this has been variously put on the Pakistanis and the Moslem fanatic forces, but the chief benefactor would seem to be the Marxists.

If the Marxists and other guerrilla groups which stand far to the left of either the Bangladesh government or the orthodox pro-Russian Communists should manage to prolong the chaos, the long-term possibility would then be that they would join with the Marxists of West Bengal in an attempt to unite the two Bengals in a new, independent and revolutionary state.

It was the fear of this development, which would cut off oil-rich Assam and Calcutta's jute industry from the rest of India, as much as the ruinous financial burden of maintaining the ten million refugees, that probably prompted Mrs. Gandhi's intervention. Her basic interest since March has been to help East Bengal's middle class to survive politically, and to prevent violent revolutionaries from taking over and teaming up with India's Calcutta-based Bengali Marxists.

Since 1967, Calcutta and West Bengal have undergone spasms of chaos, sponsored by the Marxist-controlled state government, which, replaced for short periods by direct rule from Delhi, has always been reinstalled by the local voters. The purpose of this violence—Calcutta has averaged six to eight political murders a day in the past year—has been to increase the Marxists' power. The inflow of ten million refugees and the war have helped this effort and one can predict that the same tactics will now be used in Bangladesh.

Resentment by East Bengalis of Punjabi rule has been so open and longstanding that it is sometimes asked why former President Yahya Khan agreed last year to hold Pakistan's first general elections in its twenty-three-year history, since it seemed inevitable that the Bengalis would make autonomy the issue.

To understand his action, one must retrace the history of the subcontinent's agricultural revolution, why it came so fast and why it produced the riots in early 1969 that brought down General Ayub Khan's government and forced Yahya Khan to agree to elections as the only means of insuring his military government's survival.

In late 1964, the United States State Department's Policy Planning Council . . . presented President Johnson with a study which found that the Malthusian crisis of population outstripping resources would hit the area in the mid-1970s unless something was done to prevent it. By then the American aid effort, begun under the Truman Administration's Point Four Program in 1947, had achieved some success in Taiwan, South Korea, Thailand, Mexico, Israel, Peru and elsewhere. But in India and Pakistan, whose 700 million people outnumbered the total population of the rest of non-Communist Asia, Africa and Latin America combined, the results had been disappointing. . . . [Prime Minister] Jawaharlal Nehru paid little attention to agriculture and instead used American food aid to feed his restless cities and hold down prices, while he pressed forward with rapid, state-managed industrialization. When Congress blocked funds pledged by President Kennedy for the $1 billion Bokaro steel works in 1963, Nehru turned to the Russians to build it, setting in train an increasing reliance on Moscow.

At the time, Nehru . . . [said], "Everything depends on steel. It is basic to our development." In this interview, held not long before his death, Nehru complained that, while American aid "aimed at making India self-sufficient," the amount given was only enough "to keep the country from collapsing" and not enough for it to reach self-sustained growth.

During the two decades before World War II, India, like other Asian countries, had exported its surplus grain, mostly from Punjab, to Europe. After the war, it joined other poor countries as an importer. By 1960, the net grain export to the poor countries from the United States was 19 million tons a year; by 1966, it was 36 million tons, with India taking a third. As Orville Freeman, agriculture secretary to Kennedy and Johnson, . . . [said] in 1969, "Food was used as a disposable item, with little regard for its effect on demand and prices."

After the first Indian-Pakistani war, when both countries suffered consecutive monsoon failures in 1965 and 1966, President Johnson responded with a "short-tether" policy of supplying food aid only for a few months at a time and tying it to specific action by recipients to grow more food of their own. Freeman was sent to India to negotiate an agreement with its agriculture minister . . . who needed leverage to get a shift in investment priorities through India's ruling Congress party. This American pressure worked.

Nehru died in May 1964, just a few months before the new dwarf wheat and rice seeds were planted on two hundred test acres in Asia. By 1969, the seeds were sown on 34 million acres in a belt stretching from Morocco to Java, but mostly in India and Pakistan. In the tropics, wheat and rice had been examples of Darwin's natural selection: the surviving strains had been tall, thin-strawed plants, able to keep their heads above water if flooded and to compete with weeds for their share of sunlight. When fertilized, they tended to become top-heavy and to fall over before the grain ripened.

The Japanese isolated a dwarfing gene which produced a sturdy, short-strawed wheat capable of carrying a heavy head of grain. The dwarfing gene was brought to the United States in 1947 and later incorporated with local breeding strains to produce a successful dwarf variety which had world-record yields in the Pacific Northwest. The major breakthrough finally came in Mexico, when Dr. Norman Borlaug, who has since won the Nobel Prize, produced a dwarf wheat adapted to Indian and Pakistani growing conditions. In 1962, the Ford and Rockefeller foundations joined forces in the Philippines to produce a similar dwarf rice. India imported 250 tons of the new Mexican wheat seed in the 1965 crop year and 18,000 tons in 1966; Pakistan imported 350 tons in 1965 and 40,000 tons in 1967. The green revolution was on.

Between 1967 and the eve of the Bengali war, the Pakistani Punjab doubled its wheat harvest in the most spectacular advance in grain production in human history. A record rice harvest also brought Pakistan into the market as an exporter. Across the frontier, India did almost as well, its wheat production climbing 50 percent between 1965 and 1969; mostly because of increases in the Punjab, India will probably become self-sufficient in grain next year, ending its long dependency on US surpluses.

In a purely technological sense, the transformation of the Punjab's wheat production was a great success story. Together with Ayub Khan's policy of giving private enterprise its head, it put Pakistan in seventh place, just after Spain, in the rate of growth of its gross national production. Last year [1971] the dwarf wheat was planted on 10 million of Pakistan's 15 million irrigated acres; 70,000 tractors, 7,000 threshing machines and more than 100 combines have appeared in just the last two to three years in the Punjabi fields.

As early as 1969 . . . predictions [were heard] at World Bank headquarters in Washington that agricultural success in the Punjab, coming at the same time as continued rural decline in Bengal, would contribute significantly to the breakup of Pakistan, especially as average incomes in the Western wing had abruptly risen two-thirds higher than in Bengal.

The fall of Ayub Khan's government, after weeks of urban rioting by uprooted landless laborers and small farmers, first revealed that the modernization of agriculture in the Punjab had not only sharply increased food production but also the number of unemployed peasants. The negative effect of the new methods on the poorer rural classes was more severe on the Pakistani side of the frontier, where the land ownership ceiling was 250 acres; it was 30 acres in the Indian Punjab. Pakistani government statistics claimed that only 15,000 farmers owned holdings larger than 150 acres, but did not emphasize that a great many of these properties were vast estates of 1,000 to 1,500 acres. One large landowner, who had 1,500 acres of irrigated wheat, . . . [said] that he had cleared a net profit of more than $100,000 on his last crop. While there had been some land reform under Ayub Khan, it clearly had not gone far enough.

By tradition, landless laborers in the old Punjab had received every twentieth bale of wheat harvested—enough to feed their families for a year. In India, where some adjustment had been made, they were getting in 1969 the twenty-fifth to thirtieth bale, which was an improvement. But in Pakistan they were still getting the same old absolute amount, but now by weight, instead of a percentage of the crop, and most landless laborers were being paid the same average yearly incomes of less than $100 that they had been getting for a decade.

In the 1970 election, Sheikh Mujibur Rahman and his Awami League campaigned on a straight regional autonomy issue and it was thought certain in Rawalpindi that they would sweep East Bengal. The election result which really shook the West Pakistanis was the overwhelming victory of Zulfikar Ali Bhutto and his Pakistan People's Party, which got twice the number of votes expected and virtually eliminated the conservative Islamic parties.

The middle classes feared that Bhutto, a political opportunist, had made too many promises to the poorest peasants, stirring them up and filling them with dangerously high aspirations. They did not fear Bhutto himself or his party since he and most of the other leaders are big landowners and the army has many close links with the landed families. . . . [In] rural Pakistan at the time of the elections . . . the villages were ablaze with rumors of peasants rebelling against landlords and incidents of forcible land seizure. The mood was ugly and utterly unrelated to the possibility that the Eastern wing would seek autonomy, if not independence.

Within a day of the election, one of Bhutto's top aides issued a public statement denying rumors that Bhutto favored a 50-acre land ceiling. He said that it was official party policy to support a 150-acre ceiling. In a country of 60,000 villages, where only 15,000 really big landlords would be affected, Bhutto's land redistribution proposals were obviously inadequate. The experience in the Indian Punjab has established that a farmer with 25 acres who capably manages his resources can do well with the new seeds and methods of cultivation.

Since he . . . took over the presidency of Pakistan . . . Bhutto has gone through the motions of declaring his faith in the eternal unity of the now broken state. More to the point, he has promised land, labor and educational reforms and an end to corruption and nepotism. Landowners and industrialists who refuse to cooperate have been threatened with various penalties; a few have been put under house arrest and there has been some nationalization. But with the economy down on its knees from the war, he is in no position to carry out most of the Socialist pledges he rashly made during the elections. Behind a plea for patience there has been a hint of fear that popular disillusionment may set in before his radical but badly needed policies can be implemented.

A land ceiling somewhere in the neighborhood of the Indian Punjab's thirty acres per family is essential if Bhutto's government is to survive, as are labor laws that force landlords to share a larger part of the wheat harvest with their workers. Pakistan's rush into farm mechanization must be halted in order to stem the flood of dispossessed landless laborers and small farmers into the city slums. Otherwise new waves of urban rioting are inevitable.

In Bangladesh, the future depends as much on what the Americans and Russians do as upon the Indians. The war has left India bankrupt. The 1971 budget foresaw a deficit of about $300 million; by the time hostilities broke out, it had ballooned to more than $400 million. Now it is conservatively estimated that the war will add another $200 million, even if the United States, Japan and Belgium resume economic aid, as they probably will.

If India is to be helped to survive as an open society, the place to start is Bangladesh. If the Indians, with Russian support, can restore some semblance of political stability there, massive economic and technical assistance for agriculture ought to be provided by the United States.

PARCHED LAND [4]

For two years, the rains have failed around this hamlet [in the Indian state of Gujarat—Ed.], and the relentless sun has baked the idle fields into a hard clay. Nothing grows.

Weakened by months of below-subsistence diet, villagers shuffle listlessly, their feet stirring up a fine, flour-like dust that coats everything and gives everyone the pallor of a corpse.

A few gather around a visitor to complain, and suddenly the crowd grows to a hundred pushing bodies, each shouting to make his point heard. Women are shooed away, as are children who peek at a stranger from between the bare legs

[4] From "Parched Land: In India Many Are Hungry; More Will Be Unless the Rains Come," article by William D. Hartley, staff reporter. *Wall Street Journal.* p 1+. Je. 6, '73. Reprinted with permission of The Wall Street Journal.

of their parents. "We are struggling to eat," one man says, his tattered clothes hanging over his spare frame.

The men tell of their hunger and the lack of food in government shops to satisfy it. They tell of their well, now down to just two feet of muddy water—water that must stand in pots for hours until it clears enough to drink. They tell of the rupee or two they earn each day on government make-work projects—money that isn't sufficient to buy food even when it is available.

"Sometimes we eat only once a day," one man says. "But we are happy with what we get." A few of the others look at him quizzically. "We have to be," he adds, "We're not going to get any more." The crowd laughs.

The Verdict

Then an elder quietly pronounces the verdict: "If there is no monsoon, we will die." No laughter this time—only muted sounds of agreement as the fatalistic Indian peasants consider their precarious future.

If the monsoon fails . . . If the monsoon is good . . .

These phrases are heard over and over in India as the crucial time nears this month when the monsoon should sweep up from the south, water the arid lands and free India from the grip of one of its worst droughts and famines. Everything depends on the monsoon rains that may or may not strike India soon. It has begun to rain at the southern tip of India—a good sign. But it did so . . . [in 1972], then the monsoon perversely veered into the Arabian Sea, and most of the precious rains were lost.

Two consecutive monsoon failures (three in some areas) have turned huge sections of the subcontinent into arid plains—vast spans of dry, brown land without a blade of grass, where mirages shiver in the blinding heat and seeds die in the ground. One of these sections is . . . up the coast from Bombay around this village in the state of Gujarat, where the nation bulges sharply to the west. The millions in the state of Maharashtra, east of Bombay, and the state of Rajasthan, north of here, are severely hurt. Bits and pieces of other states are also suffering.

A government official calculates that 220 million of India's 550 million persons are affected by the drought—some 80 million of them extremely hard-hit.

Other Areas Affected

Other nations have been threatened by famine, including India's neighbor Bangladesh. Food shortages—some caused by drought, others by flood—are found also in parts of Africa, the Philippines and China.

But the situation in India appears to be the worst of all, and it has had a profound effect on this nation's stability. The government insists that there really isn't any food crisis at all, and to some degree, its attitude is correct, for late-moving supplies have at least prevented mass death. Still, conditions are much worse than New Delhi will admit—as evidenced by mobs that loot "fair-price stores, where government-procured food is sold, by refugees who flood into Bombay and other big cities in search of food and water, and by riots that have wracked many cities in the worst-hit areas. In some villages, relief workers report, water sells for up to ten rupees (about $1.39) a bucket. Gold flows into Bombay as the richer landowners sell their wives' gold bracelets to buy food.

Observers say that the government is trying to promote calm and discourage food hoarding but add that its hopes rest entirely on the monsoon. Even if the monsoon is good, it will be five months before fresh crops can be harvested; yet the government is convinced it can persevere if the rains bring hope to the peasants. "If the monsoon doesn't come or is weak, Lord help us—it is going to be desperate. There just isn't enough food to be had in the world," says . . . a Ford Foundation agriculture expert.

Whether or not the monsoon comes, India intends to fight its own battle—without foreign assistance. Buoyed by victory in the war with Pakistan in December 1971, India has determined to go it alone and has rejected any further food aid from the United States and other nations.

No More Begging

"Self-reliance became a phrase constantly repeated," a foreign relief-worker says. "The Indians would rather get to rock bottom than beg again. It would be humiliating to turn to the United States again." India's pride has forced it to the international market in recent months instead of asking for aid. As a result, it spent $200 million of hard-won foreign exchange to purchase 2 million tons of wheat and grain sorghum.

India, of course, has been synonymous with famine and drought, and the history of this land is spotted with times of mass starvation. In the early 1940s, during a prolonged drought, as many as three million persons may have died in the region of Bengal. This time the government says there haven't been any starvation deaths—"a miracle," proclaims Gurucharen C. L. Juneja, secretary of food in the Ministry of Food and Agriculture. That, foreign experts say, is quibbling. Few people die of starvation, anyway, they contend, but it is always a major contributor to the actual cause of death, which is often pneumonia.

In a village here in the state of Gujarat, several women heading for a funeral are stopped and asked what their friend died of. "They said it was tuberculosis," says the eldest, a toothless, withered crone. "But she died of not getting enough to eat. So did her husband. He died four months ago."

For some years, production of grain—which accounts for about three quarters of all food—has been rising, spurred by the success of the "green revolution"—high-yielding seeds and more concentrated use of fertilizer and irrigation. Production of wheat, which benefits most from the new techniques, has more than doubled in a decade. Only a few years ago, Indians were predicting—with some justification, foreign experts say—that the country would soon reach self-sufficiency. A few adventurous souls were even talking of the nation's becoming an exporter of agricultural products.

From a low point of 72 million metric tons of grain in the mid-1960s, the time of the last major famine, production climbed steadily, reaching 108 million tons in the 1970-1971 crop year. Then the rains failed, and production dropped to 104 million tons . . . [in 1972]. The government predicts 100 million tons for the year ending . . . June 30 [1973]—a figure that some consider optimistic. . . .

The irony is that . . . there probably is enough food in India now to feed, however minimally, the areas hit by drought—provided the food can be found and moved. Like the "if" of the monsoon, however, this is a major imponderable.

Other observers feel that a degree of official bumbling and private greed, of official stubbornness and private distrust of government, combined with the devastating effects of the drought, leaves questionable the government's contention that it can feed the millions of people who live in areas where no crops are growing.

The Power Shortage

The lack of rain, of course, means there isn't enough water for crops. But equally important is the fact that nearly 40 percent of India's power is from hydro stations. So lower water levels mean that there isn't enough electricity to pump water from wells where there is some for irrigation. The shortage of power, which a US engineer here calls critical, also curtails production of fertilizer plants. These plants are hurt, too, by periodic strikes and an incredible lassitude toward maintenance. the engineer says.

Food supply in India is further complicated because 70 percent of the people live on the land, and much of what they grow is retained for their own use. Only a third of production goes to market, and that comes from just a few surplus areas, such as the state of Punjab, north of here, which is a massive supplier of wheat. "So little comes to market," one authority says, "that if you have an area suddenly not producing anything, it is pretty hard to divert the supply."

Food distribution is also hampered by a bitter battle between the government and farmers. . . . [In April 1973] the government nationalized the wholesale distribution of wheat. Previously, most of the grain that the farmers didn't use themselves was sold privately—at a usually high and negotiable price. Now, the farmers are required to sell the bulk of their surplus to the Food Corporation of India, the government agency that moves food around the nation. The price is 76 rupees (about $10.50) for 220 pounds (called a quintal) of "fair-average quality" wheat. The government takes a loss in transportation and other charges and sells it to fair-price shops for 78 rupees, which in turn retail it for 83 to 85 rupees.

Criticizing the Program

This nationalization has come under intense criticism. . . . A former food and agriculture minister has charged that "the government has neither the expertise nor the machinery to handle this complex trade." An industrialist in Bombay mutters, "Everything the government touches turns to stone."

Farmers complain bitterly that 76 rupees isn't enough when other prices are soaring (foreign agricultural experts tend to think the price fair). It is believed that farmers, indifferent to hunger elsewhere, hold back their grain, figuring that the government will have to raise the price if it wants to prevent millions from starving. (One reason the government banks so much on a good monsoon is that if the hoarding farmers anticipate a good crop, they probably will unload what they have secreted.)

"Farmers are selling enough to meet their financial obligations," one agricultural specialist insists, "but there isn't any question that they are holding back what they don't need to sell." And so the lines lengthen at the fair-price shops. The villagers wait hours in the burning sun to get their rations of wheat to grind into flour, mix with water and bake into the gritty, pancake-shaped "chapati," which is the staple of their diet. All too often, the shops run out of grain before everyone is served. "Grain from the fair-price shops is utterly insufficient," says . . . a Jesuit who directs Catholic relief-service operations in this state.

To its credit, the government isn't sitting entirely idle. The railroad system, though never very efficient even in the best of times, is practically on a war footing moving grain south from the Punjab. And New Delhi embarked some months back on a massive public-works program, not unlike that in the United States during the Depression. "The main reason we have this work is to keep people peaceful and calm," says . . . [an] Indian Catholic priest who works in this area. "If there isn't any work, they will revolt, fight, steal things."

Meanwhile, farmers plow their barren fields over and over to break up the sun-hardened clay. Many cattle have died or are hardly strong enough to move. The government has brought in water and fodder to keep some alive, for without the bullock, the farmers never will be able to work their fields, rain or no. Some who cannot feed their cattle let them wander away, just so they will die out of sight.

Water continues to grow scarcer, and hundreds of villages in this state receive water by tanker. In most, there is still enough to drink, but it is jealously guarded. Some men have dug their own shallow wells into which a little moisture seeps, and nightly they padlock wooden doors covering them.

In a remote village in the mountains of the southern part of this state, the only source of water for three hundred persons is a trickle off a hillside. It rolls across a leaf and drips into a small pot, filling it after a half-hour.

In this village, people have begun to eat the tiny packets of grain seed they usually save for the next sowing—meaning no crops for them even if the monsoon rains are good. Thousands in this state visit the dried-up lakes and dig for the shriveled roots of water reeds for food.

Malnutrition is increasing. Relief workers report seeing the distended bellies of children in the grip of protein insufficiency. Deficiency of vitamin A is widespread, and because of this in the small village of Kalak, not far from here, about six hundred Harijans (or untouchables) are blind. Most are children.

INDIA'S PLANNING GOES AWRY [5]

[Indian] President V. V. Giri, in his inaugural address to parliament early last year [1972], asked the Indian government to strive for economic independence. That government, buoyed by a military victory over Pakistan and a record food production in the preceding year, not only pledged itself to achieve this goal as soon as possible, but also began cutting old economic ties with foreign countries, especially in the West.

The agreement for imports from the United States under the Food for Peace program was terminated. Imports of fertilizers, machinery and other equipment were curtailed. A squeeze was put on foreign companies in India, particularly Western oil companies, to discourage their expansion. Previously negotiated collaborations were abruptly halted.

The government also announced that henceforth all basic industries, such as steel, fertilizer and chemicals, would be reserved for the public sector and that in the existing major industries now in private hands the government would insist on joint management. Generally, it was made known, there would be increasing state control of the Indian economy.

By year-end, however, government officials found that things were not going the way they had planned. For ex-

[5] From article by Kasturi Rangan, correspondent. New York *Times.* p 47. Ja. 21, '73. © 1973 by The New York Times Company. Reprinted by permission.

ample, the government had not expected the near-disaster on the food front that resulted from the failure of monsoon rains in several states. Output slumped by at least nine million tons from the previous year's record of 109 million tons. As a result there was widespread famine in four western states and prices of almost every commodity soared.

Officials are now frantically negotiating with food-surplus nations for at least two million tons of grains to stave off starvation and are striving to control food prices that have risen by 30 percent in the last six months.

Lower water levels led to a sharp fall in power production and many states had to impose power cuts of up to 70 percent. Many of the nation's industries, already plagued by a scarcity of raw materials and labor troubles, were further hurt.

One major factor that adversely affected the Indian economy was the withdrawal of American aid. The Nixon Administration, in the wake of India's military intervention in East Pakistan, now Bangladesh, suspended all assistance to India, resulting in the cancellation of orders placed by Indian industries for vitally needed components. Many projects dependent on American help were dislocated.

This was somewhat offset by the strengthening of ties with the Soviet Union after the signing of a twenty-year friendship treaty. While the Russians have collaborated with selected Indian state-owned projects, such as steel, heavy-machine building and oil production, India was left to find outside help for other modern industries such as fertilizers and chemicals.

As officials began worrying about a serious setback to the green revolution in rice because of a lack of fertilizers, the government reversed its policy and allowed Japanese collaboration in setting up five new fertilizer plants. Necessity may also restore American collaboration.

"Our policy has to be based on pragmatism," said an official explaining the change. This pragmatism was also evident in recent Indian overtures toward Washington and the back-pedaling on involvement with the Soviet Union.

India's $70 billion five-year plan—starting next year [1974]—was originally designed to dovetail with a Soviet five-year plan. This would have made Indian development totally dependent on Soviet needs and support. However, Prime Minister Indira Gandhi seems to have given up this idea.

"We shall evolve our own type of socialism," Mrs. Gandhi said recently. "We do not want to be the carbon copy of another country."

Thus, the Indian five-year plan is now being modified to give priority to development programs that would make India self-sufficient by using her own resources. A vast irrigation network has been mapped to free Indian agriculture from the vagaries of monsoon rains. Less than 30 percent of the total cultivable area now has irrigation facilities.

Indian foreign trade was an indirect beneficiary of the suspension of Western aid. As the nation was forced to curtail imports, a whole new market, Bangladesh, was opened and Indian exports of textiles, engineering goods and coal increased.

New projects are being promoted to absorb the millions of unemployed. This year [1973] one tenth of the 5 million educated unemployed are expected to be provided with jobs.

Nevertheless, the nation's biggest problem continues. Despite heavy government spending on the promotion of birth control, the population—now . . . [570] million—is steadily rising at a rate of almost 15 million a year. Demands for more food, housing and jobs outstrip whatever development is achieved and more and more people are pushed below the poverty line. According to a recent official estimate, 40 percent of the population lives at subsistence level without adequate food, housing or employment. Critics of Mrs. Gandhi have started taunting her for raising the slogan "End poverty," that enabled her party to sweep . . . [the 1972] elections.

"These critics seem to think that poverty could be eliminated in one or two years," she said in reply. "This is a long road and a somewhat slow road. You cannot pick it up and throw it outside your house or country as you would throw out some unwanted material."

IV. BANGLADESH, PAKISTAN, AND SRI LANKA

EDITOR'S INTRODUCTION

Much of what applies to India in the economic sense also applies to Bangladesh and Pakistan. In both countries, large numbers of people live at a subsistence level and agricultural production struggles to keep pace with the large annual population increases. For Sri Lanka (formerly Ceylon), which is much smaller and more favorably endowed by nature, the burden is less serious, although the island nation too has a population problem.

Bangladesh is in a precarious situation. The land is low-lying and criss-crossed by rivers so that devastating floods are a regular occurrence. There is little industry and few raw materials are to be found in the land (the major exception is an ample supply of jute, which is used in making burlap). To aggravate the woes of Bangladesh, the 1971 war and rebellion resulted in large-scale destruction of the area's meager resources. Hundreds of bridges were ruined. Roads were blown up. Among the large number of people killed were many in the educated class, and thus the country's scant force of trained manpower was depleted.

The first two articles in this section focus on Bangladesh. The first selection describes the scene in the early months of the country's existence, whereas the second depicts the country one year after independence. It is clear that independence—the realization of political aims—has brought with it problems of overwhelming proportions.

Pakistan, by contrast, appears to be relatively better off. In the 1950s and 1960s, in fact, Pakistan made reasonably good economic progress, even if its political progress turned out to be less than satisfactory. In some respects, Pakistan is better off now than when East Pakistan was part of the nation.

The third and fourth articles in this section relate what has happened in Pakistan (that is, West Pakistan). The first extract reviews the political and economic scene through 1966. The second recounts what has happened in Pakistan since the loss of Bangladesh (East Pakistan). This article speaks of land-reform legislation and notes that it has not been effective. Land reform is one of the most basic and difficult issues confronting the agricultural societies of south Asia and is as much an issue in India as it is in Pakistan.

The section ends with an article outlining political and economic developments in Sri Lanka.

BANGLADESH: THE FIGHT FOR SURVIVAL [1]

Even to the poets who have so eloquently sung its praises, "Golden Bengal" has sometimes seemed a living hell. For centuries, famine, disease and civil strife have visited the land as regularly as the monsoons that lash its coast. But nothing in this ancient and bitter legacy prepared the Bengalis for the calamities that have befallen them in recent months: a devastating cyclone, the insensate massacres carried out by West Pakistan's army of occupation and, finally, a savage war. And while they emerged from this baptism of death as the proud inheritors of a newly independent nation, the Bengalis' suffering is far from over. For now, another tragedy looms—the specter of an internal collapse that could conceivably lead to revolution, anarchy and the destruction of the fledgling state of Bangladesh.

Instead of alleviating their suffering, independence has in fact only brought the Bengalis new adversities. For Bangladesh emerged from war a ravaged nation. Its economy lies in collapse, its fertile farmlands are trampled and barren and its treasury is bankrupt. More than a million and a half

[1] From article in *Newsweek*. 79:35-9. Mr. 27, '72. Copyright Newsweek, Inc. 1972, reprinted by permission.

people have died—and still the killing goes on. Though the new government of Bangladesh is led by a revered national hero, Sheikh Mujibur Rahman, it has so far proved inept and unequal to the Gargantuan tasks at hand. And with the exception of the Soviet Union, which has launched an effective campaign to carve out a new sphere of influence in Bangladesh, the developed nations of the world have been either indifferent to the plight of Bangladesh or clumsy in their attempts to alleviate it.

What is most baffling about all this is that, although a number of respected voices have been raised in alarm, the world as a whole has failed to grasp the magnitude of the new tragedy that threatens Bengal. "Seventy-five million people have been caught in this upheaval," says . . . the Swiss director of the United Nations Relief Operation in Dacca. "There are no yardsticks for measuring it. Previous disaster relief operations around the world faced nothing so immense." Yet, the United States not only maintains that no catastrophe is in sight, but has actually canceled more than 60 percent of the humanitarian aid it had previously earmarked for Bangladesh. . . .

The Nixon Administration contends that additional emergency aid to Bangladesh is unnecessary because the threat of famine no longer exists. But the fact remains that the economy of Bangladesh—and thus the livelihood of the Bengalis—is in shambles. Industry lies idle, with much of its machinery ruined or ransacked and without the raw materials available to begin even modest production in those plants still capable of functioning. More than four hundred factories owned by West Pakistanis or their collaborators before the war have been abandoned, and Bangladesh is empty of skilled men to run them. Virtually the entire transportation and communications infrastructure of the country has been destroyed. Some five hundred road and rail bridges were blown up during the prolonged fighting and 7,000 of

the country's 8,000 trucks are wrecks. All in all, there is
hardly any way that vital foodstuffs can be distributed in
the countryside. . . .

Making the picture even bleaker is the fact that many of
the supplies that have been donated to Bangladesh are
thoroughly useless. Costly air charters from West Germany
flew in 250,000 sets of long woolen underwear, worthless in
Bengal's sweltering spring heat. Hundreds of bales of hand-
me-down winter clothes from Norway sit unneeded in valuable warehouse space. Planeloads of canned herring were
flown into a country whose rivers abound with fish. Repeatedly, desperately needed money has been used to buy
the wrong items. Six million dollars would have been more
than enough to rebuild the country's two largest bridges;
but, that sum was spent on blankets. Similarly, $200,000
would have purchased enough hand pumps to decontamin-
ate thousands of wells putrefied by human remains; instead,
that amount was spent on air-freight charges for drugs, with
the result that people are now cured of cholera one day only
to contract it all over again the next day by drinking con-
taminated water. . . .

Refugees

The failure to come to grips with the chaos in Bangladesh
cannot help but take a deadly toll in the wretchedly impoverished and overcrowded country. If 40 percent of the
people of the United States were packed into Florida, the
population density would roughly equal that of Bangladesh.
And with each passing week, the situation gets worse. More
than 9.7 million of the nearly 10 million refugees who fled
to India during West Pakistan's campaign of terror have returned to Bangladesh. But in a multitude of cases, their
homecoming has been bitter; 1.6 million dwellings, each of
which, on average, sheltered a family of seven, have been
demolished, according to a UN survey. By the tens of thousands, refugees have been flooding Bangladesh's cities. More
than 175,000 jobless Bengalis arrived . . . [in one week] in

the capital of Dacca, taking squatters' rights in sordid shantytowns or living amid the rubble of ruined buildings, sleeping on the streets or in burned-out railroad cars.

Unemployed, unsheltered and underfed, these droves of humanity have hardly any chance of a better existence in the coming months. For . . . the relentless summer monsoon is expected to begin, flooding three fifths of the countryside and enhancing the chances of widespread starvation. US officials, to be sure, are dubious about such developments. One State Department specialist called the danger of starvation "possible but not probable," and added: "I've heard no anxiety in this office about mass famine." But others are not so sanguine. . . .

Violence

If . . . riots should break out, they would be but another instance of the lawlessness that has scarred every day of Bangladesh's brief existence. There are nightly firefights in the major cities, and looting has become commonplace. (One formerly wealthy man recently wandered into a police station in his underwear—all he had left after being robbed for the seventh time.) Far more serious is the ongoing persecution of the 1.5 million Biharis, much-hated northern Indian Moslems who cooperated with the West Pakistani military. . . . In the worst single outbreak of violence since independence, enraged Bengalis overran a Bihari camp near Khulna and indiscriminately slaughtered hundreds of its occupants. Compounding the general trend to lawlessness is the fact that most of the Mukti Bahini guerrillas have not turned in their weapons, and such violent extremists as Abdul Kadr Siddiqui, a man who won international notoriety by bayoneting Pakistani prisoners in public, are still running private armies.

Confronted with such myriad problems, Sheikh Mujibur Rahman's regime has so far failed to find solutions. Mujib himself puts in punishing eighteen-hour days and runs what amounts to a one-man government. His home is jammed with supplicants who besiege him even while he dresses and has breakfast in the morning; his office is awash with students asking for textbooks, men hunting lost trucks, civil servants with papers to sign. Sadly, the genial Prime Minister seems congenitally unable to turn anyone away or to admit that he cannot satisfy every request; the result is that hardly anything gets done, and many supplicants wind up bitterly disappointed. . . .

To be sure, Mujib's administration has been getting some support from its allies, most notably India, whose army was principally responsible for the creation of Bangladesh. . . . As the last Indian troops left his country, Mujib won India's agreement on two sensitive issues—his government's right to try Pakistani prisoners where there is prima facie evidence that they committed atrocities and the demand that Pakistan recognize Bangladesh before other POWs will be repatriated.

Yet relations between Bangladesh and India have soured somewhat in recent weeks, as evidenced by the rather lackluster welcome given Indian Prime Minister Indira Gandhi when she arrived . . . for talks with Mujib. During the last months of Pakistani rule, Indians smuggled out the bulk of Bangladesh's vital jute crop, thereby depriving the Bengalis of essential foreign exchange. Moreover, India also took all captured Pakistani Army equipment, although much of it had been paid for by taxes levied on the Bengalis when their state was part of Pakistan. As one resentful Bangladesh official said, "What India took as war booty actually belongs to us." . . .

Russia has wasted no time—and spared no effort—moving into Bangladesh. Before Mujib left for Moscow on a state visit . . . Soviet Ambassador Valentin Popov urged that he give Russia the contract to clear the nation's harbors and thereby facilitate the flow of relief supplies. With twenty-nine sunken ships blocking the port of Chittagong and some one hundred smaller vessels obstructing the only other port, Chalna, the project had top priority in Dacca. But Mujib still hoped that a UN-sponsored operation could do the job. Assured . . . that the UN would approve the project by the time Mujib returned from Moscow, the Bengali leader stalled the Russians. But on his return to Dacca, Mujib found that final approval had not been granted by UN authorities in New York. "Tell the UN to forget about salvage," the Prime Minister . . . [said]. "We have accepted the Soviet offer. The discussion is closed."

The Soviets obviously are hoping that by undertaking the harbor-clearance project they may pave the way toward acquiring long-term berthing facilities in the two Bay of Bengal ports—and thus have an eastern anchor for their Indian Ocean fleet. But the Russians have extended their influence in Bangladesh in other ways as well. They have offered a squadron of MIGs and a small fleet of transport planes to the young nation and have expanded their embassy staff to ninety people—many of them fluent in Bengali. . . . Everywhere in Bangladesh the Soviet presence is now visible. Communist propaganda films abound on television. The Moscow News fills Dacca newsstands and symposiums on Communism are held in outlying cities.

Lobbying

It takes little detective work to determine Russia's motives in Bangladesh. For the Soviets believe, as indeed they have said privately, that the real revolution in the Bengali nation is yet to come. And when it does, they want to insure that it is oriented toward Russian communism rather than the Chinese brand. According to the Soviet scenario, the suffering and unrest in Bangladesh will of necessity force the relatively conservative Mujib to move ever farther to the left. And just in case the Bengalis do not move toward a more radical regime on their own accord, the Soviets have been doing some lobbying toward that goal. They have been telling their local sympathizers that the working class in Bangladesh has been denied the fruits of the struggle against Pakistan while the middle class has been lining its pockets.

Many Bengalis—not the least of them Mujib himself—
seem to believe that if they can swing the United States to
their side, their problems will begin to disappear. "If you
Americans can put a man on the moon, you can do anything," the Prime Minister said recently. "I plead with you
to come to the aid of my people." But while the Nixon Administration . . . will, in all likelihood, increase American
aid—it is by no means ready to plunge into yet another Asian
commitment. For one thing, active involvement in the multi-
plying problems of Bangladesh would siphon off far too
much of the already reduced foreign-aid budget. Beyond
that, there is little doubt that Washington believes the Soviet
Union has taken on an insoluble problem that can only cause
it grief—and thus distract Moscow from creating havoc in
areas more valuable to the United States. But that these
budgetary and geopolitical considerations should be allowed to stand in the way of a massive humanitarian aid
project is by no means universally accepted.

ON FIRST ANNIVERSARY, BANGLADESH'S FUTURE STILL A QUESTION MARK [2]

Propped up by massive worldwide support, Bangladesh
has survived its first year. Now, the props are going to be
kicked away and the new nation will be put to the test of
standing on its own feet.

The main prop since India defeated Pakistan . . . December 16 [1971] and handed Bangladesh its independence has
been the United Nation's Relief Organization Dacca
(UNROD).

The organization has administered over $1 billion in re-
lief and been solely responsible for distributing 2.5 million
tons of grain.

Despite pleadings by Prime Minister Sheikh Mujib Rahman, UNROD will leave Bangladesh . . . March 1 [1973],

[2] From article by Lewis M. Simons, correspondent. Washington *Post*. p 1+.
D. 18, '72. © The Washington Post. Reprinted by permission.

just as the country will be hit by the full impact of a massive food shortage caused by this year's severe drought. The harvest is again estimated to have fallen 2.5 million tons short of requirements.

"The UN thinks the emergency is over," Sheikh Mujib said in an interview with The Washington *Post*. "It is not." [The UN's relief effort has since been extended to March 1, 1974.—Ed.].

Food is not Bangladesh's only problem. The reverse side of the food-shortage coin is overpopulation in the comparatively small territory supporting 75 million persons around the lower reaches of the Ganges River.

Another of the country's many major problems is large-scale corruption linked with the lack of trained administrators. As the province of East Pakistan, Bangladesh was run as a virtual colony of West Pakistan, one thousand miles away, and Bengalis were a relative rarity in top positions in their own country.

During the war [with India], when it still looked as if the Pakistanis might manage to regain control of the situation, White House adviser Henry A. Kissinger [now Secretary of State] was reported to have said in the minutes of secret US Government meetings leaked to the press that a Bengali nation would be "an international basket case."

UN View

The view of the UN group, expressed by one of the officials who will remain in Dacca to run normal development programs, is that "relief, like first aid, must eventually come to an end. . . ."

The two other mainstays of Bangladesh in its painful first year, the United States and India, will not provide the same breadth of support as they have until now.

"When peace comes to Vietnam," Mujib said, "I'm afraid the United States will turn all its attention to aid and reconstruction there. We are happy for the long-suffering people of Vietnam, but this is a bad thing for us."

US aid, which totaled $328 million . . . [in 1972], will drop to a maximum of $60 million . . . [in 1973], according to a US diplomatic source.

India, which contributed a budget-straining $258 million, is now suffering from its own drought and famine.

"They cannot expect one more ounce of food from us," said a senior Indian diplomat. "We have given until it hurts —severely—and now we must look after ourselves."

With wheat in worldwide shortage, Bangladesh has already gone into the commercial market and is buying 600,000 tons of wheat and rice at high cost. According to one reliable source, the government has spent about $62 million of its $200 million foreign reserves for the grain.

Half of the total has been sold by an American firm. . . . But an undetermined amount has been bought from West Pakistan and is being shipped by way of Singapore, where Pakistani markings on the bags are removed. This indicates the seriousness of the country's food crisis.

"We have had serious problems for two long years," Sheikh Mujib said. "This year we are having drought. Before that there was the cyclone, and then of course the bloody war. This has caused untold human misery to my people. We hope all people who love humanity will help us."

While the food shortage is the most worrisome of the problems facing Mujib and his countrymen as they mark the first anniversary of their liberation, the many others include:

Corruption among government officials and workers of the ruling Awami League is rampant.

Young people, disillusioned with Mujib's failure to deliver the Golden Bengal he had promised, are taking to crime, often using weapons they used against the Pakistani army during the war.

Bangladesh villagers and townspeople, repelled by corrupt workers of the ruling Awami League, have killed 550 of them in the last few months.

With the nation's first elections set for ... March 7 [1973], political violence has taken a sudden upsurge, with Awami League and opposition workers battling each other at public rallies.

Prices of food, clothing and basic commodities have leveled off after soaring to unprecedented heights ... but are still out of reach of most of the nation's 75 million people.

One year after Pakistan surrendered, 93,000 military and civilian prisoners are still being held by the "Joint Command" of India and Bangladesh. Mujib must soon decide whether and when he will hold war-crimes trials, as he has repeatedly promised his people.

Bangladesh is holding some 400,000 to 500,000 members of the Bihari minority, many of them in wretched refugee camps. Many want to go to Pakistan; Pakistan is holding between 300,000 and 400,000 Bengalis, many of whom could help the new nation streamline its bumbling civil service and strengthen its pitiable armed forces. [Since the publication of this article, there has been an exchange of some of the people held.—Ed.]

Mujib's Admission

While his ministers continue to deny that corruption has permeated the administration, Mujib has finally come around to admitting it—which could be an important step toward cleaning up government. "Of course there is corruption," he said in the interview. "Don't some people in the United States say there is corruption in the Nixon Administration? But we have begun to deal with it. We have dismissed forty-four elected members of the party and suspended senior officials. You can't change the character of a nation in one or two years. It takes a lot of time."

Some observers believe Mujib will sweep out his administration once he wins the mandate he is expected to gain in the coming elections. But a reportedly growing group of young people and peasants don't believe this.

Led by two fiery former student leaders and a hero in the Bengali guerrilla force, the group, which calls itself the National Socialistic party, is building strength in the villages of Bangladesh.

Speaking in the party's Dacca headquarters, a filthy ramshackle building in a dark back alley of the city's old town, Shajan Siraj, one of the party's three leaders, explained why he and . . . Abdur Rab split from the 700,000-member, pro-Mujib Student League. They joined Major Abdul Jalil and formed the new party.

"The government has failed completely, and that means Mujib has failed, too. He is the government. So, when you know how corrupt and inefficient they are, you know what you can expect for the future."

Siraj, a small, youthful-looking man of twenty-nine, sat among a group of colleagues, all of them looking as if they were still undergraduates at a political bull session. . . .

Opposition Strength

Should they combine in united front with the country's other ragged opposition forces, they could draw as much as 10 percent of the vote from the Awami League. "That would be a terrible blow to Mujib personally," said one high government official.

There is some evidence that the National Socialistic party is being heavily bankrolled from abroad.

During the interview with Siraj, a powerfully built man with a heavy black beard and shoulder-length oiled hair entered the dingy room. Immediately all the young party workers sprang to their feet. Speaking in rapid-fire Bengali, he cautioned Siraj not to speak to the press. That ended the interview.

The man was identified as Sirajul Alam Khan, a Bengali labor leader. He has recently been reported meeting in Calcutta with members of India's Marxist Communist party and to have received assurances of support from them.

The National Socialistic party publishes a daily newspaper and several observers believe that even Alam Khan has a superior and that funding is better than the Indian Communists could offer the young Bengali Party.

While it would be easy to dismiss the National Socialistic party, student power has long been a force to reckon with in Bengali politics. . . .

Freedom Fighters

Other young people, some of whom fought in the Mukti Bahini guerrilla force and others who declared themselves "freedom fighters" after the smoke of battle cleared, are wreaking havoc in Dacca and other cities and towns. Many people in the capital are afraid to go out after dark, even in their cars. Armed gangs of young "freedom fighters" halt drivers at gunpoint and force them to give up their vehicles. According to more than one source, many of these cars are to be found in the driveways of Awami League officials.

In the rural areas of the river-veined country, villagers are increasingly taking revenge on Awami League workers who have hoarded food grains and otherwise taken advantage of their power at the local level.

The government is unable to cope with the crime wave, either in the cities or the villages, because the police force is terribly under strength. "We even had to outfit them in Indian uniforms," Information Minister Mizanur Rahman Chowdhury said in an interview.

Other armed men wearing Indian uniforms are the troops of the recently formed Jatiya Rukki Bahini or National Defense Force. They also carry Indian assault rifles, continue to be trained by Indian officers, despite denials, and are by far the smartest troops among the country's ragtag armed forces.

According to several foreign observers, Mujib formed the Rukki Bahini from among men whose loyalty to him personally is proven. He has also formed the Jubo (Youth) League, to counter the growing anti-Mujib elements in the colleges and universities.

Price of Rice

High food prices and shortages of essential commodities have become an established fact of life. Rice, which sold for $6.50 per 70-pound measure before the war, has now leveled off at $10 after hitting a high of $14. . . .

Drugs and pharmaceuticals are in extremely short supply.

"We have nothing," a Dacca pharmacist said, "not the simplest tin of aspirins or vital antibiotics."

The shortages are affecting city dwellers and peasants alike.

"In a village, toilet paper is a luxury," said one middle-class Dacca housewife. "But to my family, it is a necessity. Now we're tearing up newspapers."

The villagers are making do with short supplies of kerosene, the basic cooking fuel, mustard oil and the one or two other mainstays of existence in rural Bengal.

One of the touchiest issues facing Mujib, both inside Bangladesh and internationally, is the pending war-crimes trials of Pakistani prisoners.

The United States and Britain have advised Mujib that trials of large numbers of the 73,000 military and 20,000 civilian prisoners would cause Pakistani President Zulfiqar Ali Bhutto unmanageable problems among his own demoralized population and could seriously damage peace negotiations on the subcontinent.

Information Minister

Information Minister Mizanur Rahman Chowdhury revealed in an interview that the government "has designated 250 war criminals and these people will be tried." Investigations are continuing, Chowdhury added.

Mujib's position on the POWs is that the "Joint Command is within its rights under the Geneva Conventions in continuing to hold them because hostilities have not stopped. There is still hostility between Pakistan and Bangladesh."

Mujib refused to disclose any details of his plans for war-crimes trials except to say, "We must hold them."

India and Bangladesh would release those POWs not found guilty of war crimes "when hostilities end," he said. "That means when Pakistan recognizes Bangladesh as a sovereign nation and when they return my 400,000 Bengalis."

Asked why he didn't negotiate with Bhutto for an exchange of "his Bengalis" and the Biharis in Bangladesh, Mujib said he was willing to let the Biharis go to Pakistan but that it was not his place to negotiate.

"We conducted a poll of the Biharis, and 153,000 opted for Pakistan, he said. "The Red Cross and the United Nations should take them to Pakistan and they should bring my Bengalis back. There is no need for me to discuss this with Mr. Bhutto."

Red Cross officials, who oversee Bihari refugee camps, said Pakistan has not exhibited any interest in receiving them.

The Biharis originally came to then East Pakistan from the Indian state of Bihar when the subcontinent was divided into India and Pakistan in 1947.

Many were accused of collaborating with the Pakistan army during the bitter nine-month liberation struggle . . . [in 1971]. Since the defeat of Pakistan, they have been given refuge under International Red Cross supervision.

An unknown number were killed by vengeful Bengalis in the early days after the war. "Now we are no longer being killed physically," said a young Bihari man in the stinking, filthy, jampacked refugee camp at Mohammadpur, a Dacca suburb. "Now we are being killed off economically, socially, and culturally."

Several Biharis in Mohammadpur and also at the barbed-wire enclosed camp at the Adamjee jute mill fifteen miles south of the city said virtually every Bihari—or "stranded Pakistanis" as they are now calling themselves—desperately wants to go to Pakistan.

Told that all but the wealthiest Biharis who had fled to Pakistan, by bribing Bangladesh immigration officials, were living in camps similar to the ones here, several young men said they could not believe it.

"How can this be?" a former schoolteacher asked. "We are Pakistanis too. Surely, our brothers would want us with them. Perhaps it is only President Bhutto who does not want us." Red Cross officials said there was "very little hope" that the Biharis could be reintegrated into Bangladesh, at least not in the foreseeable future. Camp inmates concurred. "There cannot be any jobs for us when there are no jobs for Bengalis," one former railway worker said.

However, because the railways were largely run by Biharis before the war and not enough Bengalis are trained to take over the work the government has sent more than one thousand Bihari workers back to their jobs at the Syedpur rail yards. There have been violent incidents, a Red Cross worker said, but the government has not taken any further steps.

"This government is unpredictable," he said.

What is predictable is that the government and people of Bangladesh face another year of hardship and deprivation. No serious observer any longer predicts, as many did one year ago, that the nation would collapse. Countries like this one are too close to the survival line in the best of times to collapse.

Furthermore, the government has made some gains: . . . a ninety-three-page national constitution . . . [has been] signed. Mujib appears to be committed to democratic socialism. No one has starved to death.

Mujib's Commitment

Except for hard-core opposition figures, no one doubts Mujib's commitment to his people.

One high official, not a particular fan of Mujib's, said he was told that the prime minister worked day and night. "I don't know if it's true," the official said, "but some of his friends tell me he often works twenty-two hours a day."

During his interview with this correspondent, Mujib frequently removed his heavy black-rimmed glasses and tiredly rubbed his eyes and the bridge of his nose. ...

Most critics see Mujib's greatest failing as his inability or unwillingness to delegate responsibility.

"I think what you'll see after the election is Mujib becoming a dictator," said a diplomat from a neutralist country. "He'll do it because he thinks it's the way to save the country. And God knows he may be right."

Commerce Minister M. K. Siddiqi, who was chief of the Bangladesh Mission in Washington, saw more cause for optimism in ... [1973].

Reflecting quietly in his office after signing the constitution, Siddiqi noted that this new country has "some built-in advantages." He referred to the fertility of the land and the likelihood of increasing its food output many times with proper guidance, of the recent discovery of some minerals and of the presence of significant deposits of natural gas.

Then he paused.

"But we have made a great mistake." he said. "In the euphoria of victory, we promised our people the moon. Now, there are rising expectations. How can we meet them?"

AYUB KHAN'S "BASIC DEMOCRACY" [3]

Pakistan is frequently singled out as one of the success stories of the United States Agency for International Development. Starting from scratch at independence, with few assets other than cotton and jute, Pakistan's economic prospects did not appear to be particularly bright. Eighteen years and more than $3 billion in US aid later, Pakistan had achieved an average annual growth rate of 4.8 percent in national income—a comfortable margin ahead of its high 2.8 percent a year population growth rate. It was within

[3] From "India and Pakistan," Fact Sheet no 2. In *Great Decisions 1967*. Foreign Policy Association. '67. p 17-20. Reprinted by permission from *Great Decisions 1967*. Copyright 1967 by the Foreign Policy Association, Inc. 345 E. 46th St. New York 10017.

sight of producing enough food to satisfy the requirements of its 115 million citizens, and most of the goals of the nation's second Five-Year Plan, which ended in June 1965, seemed likely to be exceeded.

Late in 1965 a series of events, triggered by the war with India, forced Pakistan to trim sail, but the record nonetheless stands as a remarkable achievement.

Even to approach self-sufficiency in food production is an outstanding feat, particularly for an underdeveloped country with the fifth largest population in the world. Pakistan's industrial growth rate outdistances that of all but a handful of countries in the "third world"; in Asia, it is second only to that of Japan. These accomplishments are all the more impressive because Pakistan is an artificial creation whose population at the outset had only one bond in common, religion. East Pakistan, formerly East Bengal, is Southeast Asian, a rice-eating, jute-growing, perpetually humid river-delta land, most of whose people speak Bengali. West Pakistan is Middle Eastern, a wheat-eating, cotton-growing, often rainless desert land whose people speak half a dozen languages, none of them Bengali. The seat of government, Rawalpindi, is in West Pakistan; West Pakistanis hold most of the jobs in the civil service and the armed forces, and own nearly all major business and industry. East Pakistan, although one sixth the size of West Pakistan—roughly the size of Arkansas—has fifteen million more inhabitants, and the jute it grows supplies the nation with most of its foreign exchange earnings.

Economy on the Move

East Pakistan was particularly hard hit by partition, which cut the area off from its natural market. It had been the raw material reservoir for the jute mills of Calcutta and did very little processing of any kind on its own. The industrial base was extremely narrow. Pakistan as a whole boasted fewer than nine hundred small factories, less than four hundred small mills to convert food crops, a few light engineering works, a large shoe factory, a fledgling cement industry and only one steel smelter.

The story is a lot different now. In the last decade agricultural production in East Pakistan has soared, due in large measure to a US-supported rural development program. Besides cotton, jute and sugar mills, East Pakistan now has a fertilizer factory, a paper mill, a newsprint factory, three dockyards, a pharmaceutical plant, a steel mill and a truck assembly plant.

Farm output has also risen in West Pakistan. Moreover, the country has achieved self-sufficiency in such areas as aluminum and brass utensils, small diesel engines and some types of electric wire and cable. Pakistan exports sporting goods, cutlery and surgical instruments, and its chemical industry is moving into petrochemicals and other synthetic fibers.

Foreign aid from the West is one of the factors behind Pakistan's remarkable progress. Under the second Five-Year Plan, which ended in 1965, roughly 40 percent—or nearly $2 billion—of the total expenditures was financed by foreign loans and grants, but private investment has been encouraged, too. The state owns and controls the railroads, telecommunications and part of the air transport industry, and manufactures all military equipment, but everything else is in private hands. Roughly 70 percent of the industrial development called for by the second Five-Year Plan fell in the private sector, and foreign entrepreneurs have been offered tax holidays and a wide range of other incentives and safeguards to encourage them to set up shop in Pakistan.

Bottlenecks

Pakistan must contend with certain basic weaknesses in the economy, notably a shortage of foreign exchange, a shortage of technical and managerial personnel, an untrained work force, inadequate transport and power facilities, and a heavy dependence on two exports—cotton and jute. Neither commodity has a guaranteed market. Demand for jute has fallen, and the cotton textile industry is highly competitive.

Pakistan has proven, however, that it can make its way, and the most serious threat to continued progress is not so much economic as diplomatic—the danger of a fresh outbreak of hostilities with India. Pakistan has still not recovered from the effects of the war over Kashmir which erupted in September 1965 and the suspension of US economic and military aid. As its defense budget soared, Pakistan was forced to cut back its projected economic development by almost one fourth, and its reserves of gold and hard currency plummeted. Moreover, the war stirred up ripples of political discontent which could at some future time erupt into a tidal wave.

The chief source of internal discontent is East Pakistan. Ever since independence the East Pakistanis have felt discriminated against by West Pakistan. They claim they are underrepresented in the central government, receive less than their rightful share of development funds and have no protection against India, which surrounds them on three sides. The conflict over Kashmir heightened East Pakistan's sense of isolation and utter dependence on West Pakistan. Had India attacked East Pakistan, its only defense would have been a single division of troops. By the time reinforcements arrived—which would have required a three-thousand-mile air or sea trip via Ceylon—East Pakistan could have been overrun. "While West Pakistan was using its American tanks and American planes to fight India for the precious 5 million Kashmiris," one East Pakistani complained, "65 million Bengalis were left to fight with their bare hands if the Indians had attacked us."

In the wake of the war East Pakistani discontent boiled over into a demand by some of its leaders for full autonomy, and the central government was faced with a full-blown political crisis.

Order out of Chaos

Crises, though rare in recent years, are nothing new in Pakistan. Whereas India had Nehru to guide it through the shoals of independence, Mohammed Ali Jinnah, the father of Pakistan, died in 1948, a year after the country was founded, and the nation's only other preeminent leader, Liaquat Ali Khan, was assassinated in 1951. For seven years the country was wracked by economic, political and regional strife. Corruption became a way of life. Governments were toppled in rapid succession as a plethora of political parties jockeyed for power. The political order continued to erode until October 1958, when martial law was imposed. Three weeks later the man responsible for administering the law, General Mohammed Ayub Khan, overthrew the government and declared himself president.

A tall, muscular fifty-nine-year-old, educated at Sandhurst, Britain's West Point, Ayub Khan was the first Pakistani to hold the job of commander in chief of the army and was subsequently appointed defense minister. In his first five years as president, Ayub Khan imposed order on the country and charted the course for Pakistan's economic growth. Refugees were moved out of the cities and resettled; the educational system was expanded; land reform legislation was passed limiting the acreage which one man could own. In June 1962 martial law was rescinded.

The new constitution which went into effect that year established a strong executive. The president is indirectly chosen by an electoral college to serve a five-year term. There are checks on his powers, but the president can rule by proclamation and make law on his own when the National Assembly is not in session. The Assembly is unicameral, its 156 seats evenly divided between East and West Pakistan. East Pakistan complains that this division deprives its somewhat larger population of proportional representation. That quarrel is one of the factors behind Ayub Khan's reservations about the utility of political parties in a developing country like Pakistan which, he claims, cannot make headway under

the "strains and stresses of the Western democratic system."
Political parties are legal, but the president can and does
hamstring their activities in a number of ways. Politicians
of the pre-Ayub era are still disqualified from running for
office.

Pakistan calls its political system a "basic democracy," a
term that derives from the eighty thousand popularly elected
Basic Democrats, each of whom represents a constituency of
two hundred to six hundred voters. The Basic Democrats
make up the electoral college which chooses the president.

Khan Versus Jinnah

In the election of January 1965 Ayub Khan ran on the
ticket of the Pakistan Muslim League party (PML). He was
opposed by the sister of the late Mohammed Ali Jinnah,
Miss Fatima Jinnah, a frail seventy-two-year-old who had
never held office but whose name guaranteed great emotional
appeal with the masses. Miss Jinnah was the candidate of the
Combined Opposition parties, an amalgam of five groups
that covered the political spectrum from extreme right to
extreme left. Her backers included many of Pakistan's intellectuals, professionals, the middle class, students and workers'
organizations.

The chief issue in the campaign, as Miss Jinnah saw it,
was "democracy versus dictatorship." Her nine-point program called for a fully democratic constitution, direct presidential elections and the curtailment of the powers of the
chief executive.

Ayub Khan's campaign, on the other hand, stressed "economic and political stability with a strong center . . . for
Pakistan's forward march" and called for democracy "based
on pragmatism rather than dogmatism."

When the votes were tallied, Ayub Khan announced that
"God has saved Pakistan." He had defeated his opponent by
a margin of almost two to one. He carried East Pakistan,
where Miss Jinnah was expected to run strong, by 53 percent.
The election appeared to give the man who has been called

the "Muslim de Gaulle" a mandate to continue his policy of strong central government under a powerful executive.

Whether the central government is strong enough to curb the drive for autonomy in East Pakistan remains to be seen. The leader of this movement, Sheik Mujibur Rahman, has proposed limiting the central government's control over East Pakistan to two fields: defense and foreign affairs. He would like to see the "flight of capital" from East to West curbed and East Pakistan permitted to engage in foreign trade on its own account.

Ayub Khan has denounced Rahman's Bengali demands as treasonous, claiming that what they really amount to is a call for independence and the destruction of Pakistan's integrity. Some observers believe there is little Ayub Khan could do to prevent the formation of a breakaway regime if that is what the Bengalis decide they want. If he made any concessions, it would be interpreted as a sign of weakness; if he decided to use force he would have to build up government troops now in the East—a long and costly operation.

One important factor influencing the future relations of Pakistan's two wings is India. If India and Pakistan were able to patch up their differences, it might ease the pressure for autonomy. East Pakistan, in any event, would feel less isolated, and its economy would profit from the resumption of normal trade. [See following article.]

PAKISTAN UNDER BHUTTO [4]

The Indo-Pakistani war of 1971 and the consequent dismemberment of Pakistan have effected fundamental changes in her internal politics and external relations. The year 1971 forms a watershed in the brief and checkered history of the country, marking the end of a phase and the beginning of a new era. It will take some time for concrete and well-defined policies to emerge from the prevailing confusion and unrest.

[4] From article by Khurshid Hyder, associate professor, University of Karachi. *Current History.* 63:202-5+. N. '72. Reprinted by permission.

On the political front, by far the most outstanding development inseparably linked with the war is the total eclipse of the political role of the army. For thirteen long years the army dominated and controlled the politics of the country with tragic and disastrous results. Except for the military defeat, it is doubtful if the army could ever have been eliminated as the determining factor in politics. There is such widespread anger and disgust at the policies of the army and the imbroglio into which it dragged the country that for many years it cannot stage a political come-back. The only contingency in which it could reacquire political control would be the total breakdown of civilian control and a law-and-order situation verging on anarchy. Short of that, the political role of the army has been effectively neutralized for a long time to come.

The other point to be emphasized is the secularization of politics brought about by President Zulfikar Ali Bhutto and his party's ascendancy at the center and in the two major provinces, Punjab and Sind. In the nineteenth century, the great Muslim reformer, Sir Syed Ahmad Khan, successfully wrested the leadership of the Indian Muslims from the hold of the orthodox divines and set them on the road to modernism. Except for the Khilafat interregnum, this trend continued to predominate Muslim politics until 1947. But soon after the death of Mohammed Ali Jinnah in 1948, there was a resurgence of the rightist parties. Lacking economic and social programs, politicians adopted obscurantist tactics and exploited religious sentiments for the furtherance of their respective political aims. It is to Bhutto's abiding credit that he launched a political party with a Socialist manifesto, thereby bringing to the fore urgent economic and social issues that are directly relevant to the teeming millions, and successfully detaching religion from politics. Despite the obfuscation and pettifogging of the rightist parties, the Pakistan People's party (PPP) swept the polls and consummated the process of political secularization initiated by Sir Syed Ahmad Khan. From now on economic issues will determine the dynamics of politics. The political survival of the rightist parties will depend on their ability to meet the challenge of rising expectations and to provide an answer to the growing economic and social problems which, after years of suppression, have burst into the open and have unsettled settled attitudes and policies.

Another prominent feature of the political scene is the fact that for the first time in twenty-five years Pakistan has a popularly elected government at the center and in the provinces. This has given the people a sense of participation in the political affairs of the country. Bhutto's peculiar techniques of announcing decisions at public meetings, seeking approval for decisions at mass gatherings, and staging spectacles like the open swearing-in ceremony at the Race Course in Rawalpindi [the former capital] have certainly created for the masses the illusion of being associated with the decision-making apparatus of the government.

Since political activity has emerged after years of military repression, there is understandably a great deal of political activism devoid of any purpose. In the circumstances, political stability and institutionalized politics are the two prime requirements of the 1970s. Under growing pressure, Bhutto reluctantly lifted martial law in April 1972—four months earlier than scheduled—and introduced the interim constitution. . . . Provincial autonomy has been conceded, but it is overshadowed by a plethora of overriding powers for the center ostensibly designed to meet various emergencies. . . . The government seems inclined towards a presidential form of government with a reasonably strong center. . . .

One of the main problems facing the framers of the constitution will be to determine the degree of autonomy to be granted to the provinces and to work out an acceptable base for center-state relations. The opposition parties, particularly the National Awami party (NAP), want a federal parliamentary system and maximum autonomy for the provinces. The secession of East Pakistan [now Bangladesh] has aroused lively apprehension about the domination of Punjab in the other three provinces. Punjab is the biggest and richest province. . . . The only way to allay these fears is to concede maximum autonomy to the provinces. Given the ruling party's preference for a strong center, there is bound to be considerable discord and friction between the government and the opposition over the form of the future constitution. It may not be easy for Bhutto to bypass the opposition parties, since they command the majority in two provinces. Moreover, even in his home province, Sind, a strong center will not be tolerated and will lead to the gradual erosion of his support.

The PPP was elected on a Socialist mandate. During the election campaign, extravagant prospects were held out to the working class promising them a bright new world free of exploitation and geared to providing maximum social and economic benefits. This naturally touched off a groundswell of expectations which, in the best of times, would have been difficult to fulfill. But in the aftermath of the war and defeat, the loss of East Pakistan, the urgent need to adjust the economy to the altered circumstances and to cope with the shortfalls and shortages created by nine months of very costly military operations in East Pakistan have made it well nigh impossible to meet the persistently rising demands of the workers.

The government has, however, made some formal gestures to check spreading unrest and to take some of the heat out of the labor discontent and agitation which had assumed alarming proportions in all industrial cities, particularly Karachi. It has taken over the management of a number of large firms but has left ownership intact, following the Economic Reforms Order promulgated in January 1972. It has also abolished the managing agency system which was regarded as an anachronism. There had been a growing pressure for its abolition, particularly after India eliminated the system a number of years ago. A new labor policy has also been announced, which promises to raise the workers' share in the profits and seeks to enlarge considerably the scope of fringe benefits. In March 1972, land reforms were announced which have reduced the maximum ceiling on individual ownership of land from 500 to 150 irrigated acres and from 1,000 to 300 nonirrigated acres. Land becoming surplus as a consequence of lowering the ceiling is to revert to the state which, in turn, is to distribute it among the landless peasants.

The aforesaid reforms and the manifesto of the PPP notwithstanding, the government and its policies are far from Socialist. Not a single industry has been nationalized. The land reforms are just an eyewash, and have not in any significant manner brought about the redistribution of land in favor of the landless peasants. The recent budget has not levied an income tax on land revenue. But given the general unrest and the revolution of rising expectations among the workers and the peasants, the government will be forced eventually to move towards greater socialization. The land ceiling will have to be lowered further; revenue receipts will be subjected to income tax, and some industries will be brought under state control. A maximum limit will have to be placed on wealth and incomes. The concept of welfare cannot be left vague and ambiguous, but will have to be given content by bold and radical policies geared to providing economic and social benefits for Pakistan's struggling and impoverished millions.

Foreign Policy

The breakaway of East Pakistan is bound to have a far-reaching impact on the direction and course of Pakistan's foreign policy. To quote Bhutto:

> The severance of our eastern wing by force has significantly altered our geographic focus. This will naturally affect our geopolitical perspective. The geographical distance between us and the nations of South East Asia has grown . . . at the moment, as we stand, it is within the ambit of South and Western Asia. It is here that our primary concern must henceforth lie.
> There is the whole uninterrupted belt of Muslim nations, beginning with Iran and Afghanistan and culminating on the shores of the Atlantic and Morocco. With the people of all these states we share a cultural heritage, religious beliefs and a good

deal of history. There is thus a community of interests which is further buttressed by the similarity of our aspirations and hopes. Clearly we have to make a major effort in building upon the fraternal ties that already bind us to the Muslim world.

It is obvious that Pakistan will from now on give top priority to the fostering of closer links with the Muslim countries. This explains Bhutto's whirlwind tour of the Muslim states in January and May 1972. The underlying aim of the overtures to the Muslim countries seems to be to evolve a consensus on the issues which face the country and to elicit their support in the negotiations with India and Bangladesh. During the 1971 war, most of these countries supported Pakistan. None of them, except for Iraq, has yet recognized Bangladesh. Relations with Libya, Jordan, Kuwait and Saudi Arabia have become particularly close in view of the aid extended by them during the war and their continuing support.

A natural corollary of Pakistan's emphasis on her links with the Muslim countries has been the reactivation of her role in CENTO [Central Treaty Organization]. For the first time since 1968, a cabinet minister was sent to the 1972 CENTO ministerial meeting in London. This represents a sharp reversal of the policy of the 1960s. Pakistan became a member of SEATO [South East Asia Treaty Organization] and CENTO as a result of the Mutual Security Agreement with the United States. When United States Secretary of State John Foster Dulles outlined his scheme for a "northern tier" defense system consisting of countries directly contiguous to the Soviet Union, attention focused on Pakistan as a possible recruit, in view of the refusal of the Arab countries to be drawn into such an arrangement. The avowed purpose of the . . . pact was to counter and contain Soviet influence in the Middle East. At that time, Pakistan was not directly or indirectly menaced by the Soviet Union and its policies; she joined the pact only to qualify for the receipt of military aid from the United States and "to forge closer relations with our neighbors in the Middle East."

However, since Pakistan joined CENTO primarily at the instigation of the United States, the loosening Pakistani-American alliance in the 1960s ineluctably influenced Pakistan's attitude towards it and she gradually deemphasized her role in it. Changes in the global power structure also made it essential for Pakistan to normalize her relations with the Soviet Union, and that, in turn, called for a reduced and passive role in CENTO. Finally, as Pakistan moved to bilateralism, CENTO seemed superfluous.

The happenings of 1971 in the subcontinent have revived Pakistan's interest in CENTO and have invested it with fresh importance. The defeat and dismemberment of Pakistan have brought about a qualitative change in the power balance. Pakistan is now much more vulnerable to combined Indo-Soviet pressures than she was in the 1960s. Diminishing American interest in South Asia is paralleled by enhanced Soviet activity, aimed at the isolation and encirclement of China and the establishment of Indo-Soviet hegemony. The Soviet Union is strongly entrenched in India and Afghanistan. Pakistan's relations with the Soviet Union—except for a brief span of five years, 1965-1970—have not been too friendly. Pakistan's alignment with the West and her membership in the pacts in the 1950s, close links with China in the 1960s, on the one hand, and the Soviet Union's special relationship with India, on the other, precluded the possibility of abiding friendship between the two countries. Ex-President Ayub Khan's visit to the Soviet Union in 1965, and the Soviet Union's nonpartisan role in the Indo-Pakistani War of 1965, followed by its active mediation between the contending neighbors at Tashkent, infused some warmth and cordiality into Pak-Soviet relations.

In the post-Tashkent period, the Kremlin seemed interested in a balanced policy towards the two adversaries. But its role in the East Pakistani crisis and its Treaty of Friendship and Cooperation with India signified a deliberate and decisive change in policy. Moscow renounced the role of an impartial arbiter in Indo-Pakistani affairs in favor of

total alignment with India, irrespective of the repercussions
of this policy on its relations with Pakistan. Soviet policy
since the war is aimed at reducing and weakening Pakistan
as a political force on the subcontinent. The developments
of 1971 have thus lent substance to what was hitherto only
a vague fear of Soviet expansion. In the 1950s, the Soviet
threat was nonexistent, or at best latent; currently it is active.
Consequently, Pakistan's interest in CENTO has been re-
activated. Pakistan may also hope to obtain military supplies
through the CENTO partners because the resumption of
American military aid on a bilateral basis seems improbable
in the near future.

Indo-Pakistani Relations

Indo-Pakistani relations have taken a turn for the better,
it seems, as a result of the recently concluded agreement at
Simla [in India]. The relations between the two countries
for the last quarter of a century have been uniformly un-
friendly. The historical rivalry between the Hindus and the
Muslims culminating in the partition of the subcontinent,
the events before and after partition, the Kashmir dispute,
conflicting foreign policies and, above all, a general feeling
in Pakistan that India had not accepted the finality of the
partition, foreclosed all possibilities of good neighborly relations. In view of the developments emanating from the
1971 war, the power balance in the subcontinent has de-
cisively and irrevocably shifted towards India. Pakistan can
no longer adhere to the policy of confrontation. It was never
a viable policy; in the altered circumstances, it has become
dangerous and irrelevant. Pakistan has been reduced by one
half. India is in occupation of nearly five thousand square
miles of Pakistani territory in the Punjab and Sind, and is
holding ninety thousand Pakistani prisoners of war. It was,
therefore, essential for Pakistan that parleys at the summit
level be initiated.

As far as India is concerned, her unequivocal victory in
the 1971 war achieved her basic aim, i.e., the breakup of

Pakistan. The Muslims of pre-1947 India are now split into three groups—those in Bangladesh, in Pakistan, and the Muslim minority in India. To all intents and purposes, Bangladesh will be a client state of India; Pakistan halved cannot pose a threat to India. India may not now be seriously interested in any confederal arrangement with Pakistan, or any other scheme of reunification that would make the Muslims a strong political force in India. Split into three more or less equal portions, they are not likely to pose a serious challenge to the Hindu domination of the subcontinent. The policy of "divide and rule" has reemerged as the guiding principle of India's policy towards Pakistan. India may thus, for the first time, be genuinely desirous of seeking an accommodation of differences with Pakistan. India is also keen to regain and revive her influence in the third world, where her prestige suffered a sharp slump on account of her policy towards Pakistan. . . .

In view of all these factors, the summit meeting at Simla in July 1972 did not end in a fiasco, but brought about an agreement on some of the issues arising from the 1971 war. According to the agreement, the two countries have "resolved to put an end to the conflict and confrontation that have hitherto marred their relations." They have also agreed to the settlement of disputes by peaceful means, to noninterference in each other's internal affairs, to the gradual resumption of communications, trade and diplomatic relations, to the withdrawal of forces to their side of the international border and to a final settlement of the conflicts over Jammu and Kashmir.

The agreement is only a first step in the process of protracted and complex negotiations to settle the dispute. After a generation of strife, the two countries have been able to edge towards a friendlier dialogue. But from Pakistan's standpoint, the agreement is far from satisfactory. In agreeing to settle disputes by peaceful means, Pakistan has been forced to accept indirectly a sort of "no war pact," which she has resisted for the last twenty-five years. The United

Nations role in Kashmir has been obscured in favour of bilateral negotiations—another clear gain for India. Troop
withdrawals are confined to international borders and Kashmir has not been included. Nothing has been settled at
Simla about the prisoners of war. Their repatriation will
have to wait till after Pakistan recognizes Bangladesh. But
a defeated Pakistan could not have hoped for anything better; one cannot lose the war and win the peace. Pakistan had
nothing to offer except professions of friendship. This is the
irreducible price she had to pay for her defeat.

The Kashmir Dispute

The Kashmir dispute has been frozen for the time being.
It will take some time before a final agreement on it can be
negotiated. Although Bhutto is prepared for a military disengagement in Kashmir, political disengagement seems difficult. Pakistani sentiment is heavily invested in Kashmir. For
the last twenty-five years, successive governments have told
Pakistanis repeatedly about the economic, political, strategic
and even ideological importance of Kashmir. All this cannot
suddenly be talked away, or set aside. Public opinion will
have to be turned gradually toward the acceptance of the un-
alterable reality.

For Bhutto the task is difficult. He is hamstrung by his
past statements. But since his coming to power there has
been a basic change in his position on Kashmir. He has suggested that the cease-fire line be made into a "line of peace"
and that it is up to the Kashmiris to fight for the right of
self-determination if they want a different future. He may
nonetheless find it difficult to agree to the formal conversion
of the *de facto* boundary into a *de jure* border. Political
pressures, particularly in the Punjab, may prevent Bhutto
from formally acknowledging the permanent division of
Kashmir.

There is a consensus that Bangladesh should be recognized. Sheik Mujibur Rahman's refusal to hold any parleys
before recognition, the insistence of his government that

war-crimes trials be held, and the question of the treatment of the non-Bengali minority in Bangladesh are creating obstacles to recognition. Once there is some understanding on these and other issues stemming from the division of the country, Pakistan will forthwith extend recognition. It is in the combined interests of both countries that diplomatic, economic and communications links should be established without further delay. Pakistan's insistence on talks before recognition and the refusal of Bangladesh to agree to such talks have created an impasse. But efforts to find a way out must continue.

US-Pakistani Relations

Pakistan's relations with the United States have become more intimate. The estrangement of the mid-1960s has given way to a renewed understanding based on an underlying identity of views on the problems which confront the subcontinent. American policy towards Pakistan during the 1971 crisis in East Pakistan was decidedly sympathetic. Throughout the long and difficult months of the civil war in East Pakistan, Washington tried to bring about a political settlement among the three contending parties and to defuse the mounting tensions on the Indo-Pakistani borders. Although Washington's efforts to promote a negotiated settlement proved abortive, its role in the Indo-Pakistani war was direct and decisive. It sponsored the cease-fire resolutions in the United Nations Security Council and the General Assembly, and forced India through the Soviet Union into agreeing to the cease-fire in West Pakistan.

The two irritants in Pak-American relations in the 1960s were Pakistan's *entente cordiale* with China and Indo-American collaboration consequent upon the Sino-Indian War of 1962. The suspension of United States military aid to Pakistan in 1965 and its total discontinuance in 1967 further weakened the rationale of Islamabad's alliance with Washington. The discontinuance of American military aid compelled Pakistan to look to the Soviet Union for the fulfilment of her defense requirements. This, in turn, weaned Pakistan away from the United States and, in 1968, prompted the decision not to renew the lease on the communications base at Badebar.

The dramatic change in United States policy towards China set in motion a series of developments which have had a profound impact on United States-Pakistani relations. The new policy removed one of the major points of discord between them. It also brought to an abrupt end the parallelism in Indo-Soviet and American policies towards China and directly led to the Indo-Soviet Treaty of Friendship and Co-operation. To offset the danger posed by the Indo-Soviet alliance, Pakistan is anxious to establish closer links with the United States. Bhutto has called for the reactivation of the Mutual Security Agreement of the 1950s and the replacement of American equipment destroyed during the course of the 1971 war with India.

However, there is no disposition on the part of the United States to negotiate a new military agreement with Pakistan; this was categorically affirmed by a State Department spokesman when he was asked to comment on Bhutto's statement. The Nixon doctrine envisages a conscious curtailment of the United States military role and its commitments in Asia; after the American military disengagement from Vietnam, there is bound to be a further narrowing and sharpening of American interests in the Asian land mass. The role of the United States in the Asian power balance will be more economic and diplomatic than military. It is, therefore, difficult to predict the extent to which the United States will be willing to reciprocate Pakistan's desire for closer links. Given the power environment in South Asia, American attitudes may be conditioned largely by the nature and degree of Soviet involvement in India and the latter's ability, or inability, to maintain balanced relations with the two superpowers. If New Delhi decides to strengthen and develop further its alliance with Moscow, Washington may find it expedient to support Islamabad. Alternatively, if India plays down the implications of her 1971 treaty of friendship with the Soviet Union and successfully maintains an equipoise in her relations with the two superpowers, the United States may avoid a special relationship with Pakistan.

Relations With China

Sino-Pakistani relations continue to be close. China extended unqualified diplomatic support to Pakistan during the war, having given substantial military equipment in the preceding months. Chinese support was friendly but cautious in the initial period of the crisis; it grew stronger and more outgoing after the Indo-Soviet Treaty but fell short of military intervention. The situation on the Sino-Soviet borders and the Indo-Soviet Treaty immobilized China's military role in the war. In addition, China had always been in favor of negotiations and a peaceful settlement of the crisis in East Pakistan and the Indo-Pakistani dispute linked with it. . . .

By unmasking Soviet expansionist designs in South Asia, the 1971 war has reinforced the need for continued collaboration between Pakistan and China. Despite Pakistan's curtailed size and importance, she can still act as a balancing factor against India and the Soviet Union. With the change in the military balance on the subcontinent (consequent upon the Indo-Pakistani war), the threat to Sinkiang-Tibet has grown and a new critical situation has arisen for China. If one examines more precisely the geostrategic situation in the border area south of Sinkiang, the reason for a Sino-Pakistani identity of interests becomes obvious. In that area, northern Kashmir forms a land bridge between Pakistan and China. The opening of the "silk route" connecting Gilgit in Kashmir and Kashghar in Sinkiang in 1970 has brightened the prospect of further cooperation between them. China's security requirements are directly affected by further developments in South Asia. She will, therefore, help Pakistan to get over her defeat by India and, with regenerated military forces, enable her to act as a check against India and the Soviet Union.

The Soviet Union

Pakistan's relations with the Soviet Union have been far from satisfactory in the past year [1972] and may continue to be intractable. Soviet diplomatic activity in South Asia has led to renewed big-power interest in the region. The Soviet Union's defense pact with India has upset the power equilibrium on the subcontinent and has ended the supervisory role in Indo-Pakistani affairs which the Soviets played with consummate skill after Tashkent. During the 1971 crisis in East Pakistan, Soviet policy was openly hostile to Pakistan and constituted an unwarranted interference in her domestic affairs.

The Soviet Union extended unqualified support to the Awami League and tried to pressure Pakistan in a number of ways. Economic aid was suspended, and Russian experts working on various projects were recalled. Military aid to India was sharply expanded. With the outbreak of the war, unequivocal military and diplomatic backing was given to India. By its repeated use of the veto, the Soviet Union successfully frustrated all the efforts of the United Nations to bring about a cessation of hostilities and to effect the withdrawal of Indian troops from East Pakistan. Soviet maneuvers to prevent direct Chinese intervention were aimed at ensuring Indian victory and bringing about the breakup of Pakistan.

Notwithstanding the Indo-centric policy of the Soviet Union, Pakistan cannot afford to antagonize the Soviet Union openly and will have to exert maximum diplomatic effort to blunt Soviet hostility even if she cannot win Soviet friendship. The Soviet Union has acquired a hegemonial position in India and Afghanistan—the two neighbors with whom Pakistan has outstanding disputes. The Soviet Union can encourage the irredentist claims of both these countries against Pakistan and provoke recurring tensions on both sides of the Pakistani border. In the immediate framework of Indo-Pakistani relations, it is imperative for Pakistan to mollify the hostility of the Soviet Union. The Soviet Union is the only country which can influence victorious India to adopt an accommodating policy towards her vanquished neighbor. On the questions of the repatriation of the prisoners of war and the war-crimes trial which Bangladesh insists on holding, Moscow, by virtue of its pervasive influence in Dacca and Delhi, can help to promote a mutually acceptable settlement.

Impelled by these considerations, Bhutto has expediently overlooked the Kremlin's role in the dismemberment of Pakistan. In March 1972, he traveled to Moscow to work out some consensus with regard to Soviet-Pakistani bilateral relations and the whole subject of a political settlement on the subcontinent. Although his visit led to the restoration of trade, economic, scientific, technological and other ties, there was considerable disagreement on the South Asian political situation. The Soviet Union continues to be interested in sponsoring a security pact in Asia to which Pakistan cannot accede, given her friendship with Peking. Pakistan is the missing link in the Soviet Union's *cordon sanitaire* round China. It will thus be in the Soviet interest to reduce and limit Pakistan's influence in South and Western Asia. The Soviet Union will try to bring about the normalization of Indo-Pakistani relations in such a way that a degree of interdependence is created between them which will eventuate in India's domination over Pakistan. This explains the frequent use of the phrase "states of Hindoostan" by Soviet Premier Aleksei Kosygin during the Pakistani president's visit to the Soviet Union. Another way of restricting Islamabad's role in South Asian affairs would be to try to promote regional dissensions in Pakistan which will inhibit her from playing an active part in developments in South Asia. Afghanistan is an effective weapon through which Moscow can promote unrest. Radio Afghanistan has, of late, stepped up propaganda on Pakhtunistan; the Afghans are also active in the tribal belt. The leaders in the Kremlin can thus, by various means, chasten and subdue Pakistan.

Pakistan's ability to resist Soviet pressures will depend largely on the extent to which China and the United States help her to resist. The attitude of the Muslim countries will be another significant factor.

A new order is slowly emerging from the ruins of the old order in Pakistan. Despite formidable problems, the government has taken its first hesitant steps toward democracy and is indecisively edging in the direction of a more equitable economic system. Foreign policy is also being reoriented to meet the challenge of the changed power balance. The present leaders must try to jolt the Pakistani people out of the despondency and frustration arising from the defeat and humiliation of 1971.

CEYLON: THE BITTER HARVEST [5]

Those who know the beauty of Ceylon [Sri Lanka] are troubled by the events that have exploded on the island. In South Asia, it is envied for its relative calm, but recent occurrences have brought it to the brink of civil war.

For two weeks in early April [1971], young radicals, many from educated middle-class and well-to-do families, controlled most of the island's rural areas and caused the government to resort to heavy military action against its own people. On April 6 the prime minister, Mrs. Sirimavo Bandaranaike, broadcast that ammunition dumps and bombs had been discovered and that a plan to attack the capital city of Colombo (and to kidnap her) had been detected; that it had been foiled, but that terrorism was unleashed in the country.

The April 5 *Times of Ceylon* had already headlined the acute overcrowding in prisons, which had become "a serious hindrance to more effective training and treatment of both convicted and unconvicted prisoners." Added to the jailing of several hundred people came the imposition of emergency curfews and suspension of civil liberties, including visas to

[5] From article by Elizabeth Gilliland, free-lance journalist. *Nation*. 212: 582-4. My. 10, '71. Reprinted by permission.

travel to Ceylon. Heavy censorship was imposed as the government sought, Chinese fashion, to isolate itself from the gaze of the world while it quelled its revolution.

As days passed and the organized character of the insurgency became apparent, the government was forced to appeal to the United States, Britain and India for aid. It notably did not appeal to the Communist bloc countries, with which it has aligned itself, though by the third week the Soviet Union was supplying manned MIG-17s. Thus the radical extremists of Ceylon had surfaced, suddenly and unexpectedly, harvesting the fruit of discontent sown by faulty economic planning and an inability on the part of the government to deal with profound social change.

The pangs of modernization in this microcosmic island society reflect something of what is taking place in much of Asia, as the population balance shifts toward higher percentages of young, nationalistic—or at least non-Western-oriented—and economically frustrated people. . . . An Asian intellectual living in the States believes that the events in Ceylon illustrate the volatility of politics in Asian nations that look calm on the surface but have the capability of exploding without warning. He says that

a covert political system, distinct from conventional politics, is evolving among those younger than twenty-three. This represents the politicizing of the first generation of educated youth whose attitudes and expectations differ markedly from those of their elders. These young people, rather than moving into the power patterns set by the older generation, tend to resort to extraparliamentary action, with the result that this second world of politics surfaces like a Mt. Etna.

Young people in Ceylon are the beneficiaries of two decades of large-scale social welfare programs—rice subsidies, free hospitalization, and perhaps most important, free education from kindergarten to university. The rise in the number of educated can be traced directly back to the establishment of free schooling—compulsory to sixteen—in 1942. This schooling has produced a growing problem for the government, which in its planning would like to be able to count on more farmers and laborers. It could in fact create jobs rather easily in these categories, and begin to tap some of the manpower resources by providing economic opportunity, but there are few takers. People who have been educated in the free schools and the University of Ceylon prefer not working at all to taking jobs as domestics or laborers.

Of the 13 million Ceylonese, some 50 percent of the adults are unemployed and many more, especially women, are underemployed. But this high rate has not been as serious a problem in Ceylon as is the 6 percent unemployed in the United States. Historically, the family has been the base of life in Ceylon. People have sustained themselves within a family group and it is not thought necessary that everyone be employed. Certainly it is no disgrace to be without work, and no one will starve on an island where nature is so kind....

Traditional attitudes have changed and unemployment has become incendiary. But in the elections of May 1970 it was apparently not an issue that influenced the electorate to any large degree, nor did there seem to be a threat that the Communists might capitalize on the situation, as they have tended to do where there is unrest....

What did happen in the elections was that a coalition party came to power that includes both Trotskyists and Communists (terms used in ways not easily equated with their Western counterparts) within a Socialist-oriented government. Of the sixteen cabinet members one is a Communist, but only a handful of Communists were elected to the British-patterned parliament. Youth supported the election of Mrs. Bandaranaike and the United Front Group, but within less than a year have swung away from their allegiance to the point of executing civil war.

Soon after Mrs. Bandaranaike and her party took over, a new direction in foreign policy was inaugurated. The government recognized North Korea, North Vietnam and the Vietcong "shadow" regime and withdrew recognition of

Israel. What this implied was an attempt to gain moral support and material assistance from the Socialist bloc and, within the claimed framework of nonalignment, to reverse the more pro-West orientation of the previous regime.

Materially this has meant little if anything to Ceylon, and the impact on the so-called world balance of power cannot be great. Ceylon continues a sixteen-year trade relation with mainland China in which China buys rubber, paying a price above the world level, and sells rice to Ceylon below the market. The withdrawal of recognition of Israel has had some impact because of Ceylon's tea markets in the Arab world. . . .

The need for foreign technology is crucial in Ceylon, which is attempting to become self-sufficient in food by growing more of its own crops. The "green revolution" has affected the country, but in a limited way. Gentleman farmers have adopted tractors and chemical fertilizers. The peasants, however, when they have gotten hold of these items of modern technology, have found it more profitable to sell them to the gentleman farmers for immediate cash returns than to use them to improve their own output. Diversification of crops has been encouraged in this rice-growing country, and it may be that new crops such as onions and potatoes will cut down on reliance on imports.

When asked about foreign investment, before the outbreak of violence, people from Ceylon would say that it is needed. Aside from the ostensible benefits of technology, they said, the simple reason is that more external capital flows are needed for the country's development. So far, however, the new government has not announced plans to promote interest among foreign companies, and political uncertainty, nationalization threats, and a foreign policy oriented toward the Communist bloc have reduced external (Western) investment to a trickle.

Despite allegations to the contrary, the leaders of Ceylon have shown an increasing awareness of the need for the people to develop according to their own tradition and through

use of local skills and creativity. A World Bank loan of
$10 million for highway maintenance was recently rejected
by the minister of Irrigation, Power and Highways because
the Bank insisted that nine of the eighteen bridges planned
be built by foreign contractors. Terms of this aid are now
in the process of renegotiation. In an illuminating aside, the
minister remarked that roads built in Ceylon should not be
on the model of American expressways.

Tourism could be a major source of foreign exchange
earnings, but many islanders fear it because of the predictable accompanying problems—gambling, prostitution and
commercialism. Also the influx of affluent people to luxury
hotels would have a bad effect on Ceylon's largely rural society. As one man said, "We do not want to become a country of waiters and busboys." . . .

Effective economic planning and a leadership that can
evoke forces of constructive change are desperately needed
in Ceylon as the nation tries to do in one generation what
took the West three centuries—to move from feudalism into
the modern world. Although the people have been deeply
concerned about the problems that an increase of industry
brings—and anyone from a technologically advanced country can understand this concern—it offers at least a partial
answer. But in the immediate context, the answering of
force with force seems to be the government's only recourse
for dealing with what one hopes will be a short-lived bitter
spring.

BIBLIOGRAPHY

An asterisk (*) preceding a reference indicates that the article or a part of it has been reprinted in this book.

BOOKS, PAMPHLETS, AND DOCUMENTS

Barnds, W. J. India, Pakistan, and the great powers. Praeger [for the Council on Foreign Relations]. '72.
Basham, A. L. The wonder that was India; a survey of the history and culture of the Indian subcontinent before the coming of the Muslims. Taplinger. '68.
Beny, W. R. Island Ceylon. Viking. '71.
Bhatia, Krishan. The ordeal of nationhood; a social study of India since independence. Atheneum. '71.
Bolitho, Hector. Jinnah: creator of Pakistan. Macmillan. '55.
Brecher, Michael. Nehru: a political biography. Oxford University Press. '59.
*Brown, W. N. The United States and India, Pakistan, Bangladesh. 3d ed. Harvard University Press. '72.
Carstairs, G. M. The twice born; a study of a community of high-caste Hindus. Indiana University Press. '58.
Fischer, Louis. The life of Mahatma Gandhi. Harper. '50.
Fodor, Eugene, ed. Fodor's India, 1973; a definitive handbook of the Republic of India. McKay. '73.
*Foreign Policy Association. Great Decisions (1967). The Association. 345 E. 46th St. New York 10017. '67.
        Reprinted in this book: Excerpts from Fact Sheet no 2, India and Pakistan. p 17-20.
Frankel, F. R. India's green revolution; economic gains and political costs. Princeton University Press. '71.
Galbraith, C. A. and Mehta, Rama. India now and through time. Dodd. '71.
Galbraith, J. K. Ambassador's journal. Houghton. '69.
Gordon, L. A. and Miller, B. S. A syllabus of Indian civilization. Columbia University Press. '71.
Harrison, S. S. India: the most dangerous decades. Princeton University Press. '60.
Isaacs, H. R. India's ex-untouchables. Day. '65.

*Isenberg, Irwin. The Indian subcontinent. Scholastic Book Services. '72.

Jahan, Rounaq. Pakistan: failure in national integration. Columbia University Press. '72.

Karunatilake, H. N. S. Economic development in Ceylon. Praeger. '71.

Kaul, B. M. Confrontation with Pakistan. Barnes & Noble. '72.

Kaushik, Devendra. Soviet relations with India and Pakistan. Harper. '71.

Khan, A. R. The economy of Bangladesh. St. Martins. '72.

Lewis, J. P. Quiet crisis in India; economic development and American policy. Doubleday. '64.

Lewis, Oscar and Barnouw, Victor. Village life in northern India; studies in a Delhi village. University of Illinois. '58.

Loshak, David. Pakistan crisis. McGraw. '72.

Markandaya, Kamala. The coffer dams. John Day. '69.

Markandaya, Kamala. Nectar in a sieve. John Day. '55.

Maxwell, N. G. A. India's China war. Cape. '70.

Mehta, V. P. A portrait of India. Farrar. '70.

Moraes, D. F. The tempest within; an account of East Pakistan. Barnes & Noble. '72.

Moraes, Frank. Witness to an era. Holt. '74.

Morehouse, Ward, ed. Science and the human condition in India and Pakistan. Rockefeller University Press. '69.

Myrdal, Gunnar. Asian drama; an inquiry into the poverty of nations. Pantheon. '68.

Nair, Kusum. Blossoms in the dust; the human factor in Indian development. Praeger. '62.

Neale, W. C. India: the search for unity, democracy and progress. Van Nostrand. '65.

Nehru, Jawaharlal. The discovery of India. Doubleday. '60.

Palmer, N. D. The Indian political system. Houghton. '71.

Papanek, G. F. Pakistan's development; social goals and private incentives. Harvard University Press. '67.

Segal, Ronald. The crisis of India. Cape. '65.

Siddiqui, Kalim. Conflict, crisis and war in Pakistan. Praeger. '72.

Singer, M. B. When a great tradition modernizes: an anthropological approach to Indian civilization. Praeger. '72.

Singh, Patwant. India and the future of Asia. Knopf. '66.

Spate, O. H. K. and others. India, Pakistan and Ceylon; the regions. Methuen (distributed by Barnes & Noble). '72.

*Talbot, Phillips. Understanding India. (Headline Series no 214) Foreign Policy Association. 345 E. 46th St. New York 10017. '73.

Wallbank, T. W. A short history of India and Pakistan. New American Library. '62.
  Abridged edition of India in the new era.
Ward, Barbara. India and the West. Norton. '61.
Wheeler, R. S. The politics of Pakistan; a constitutional quest. Cornell University Press. '70.
*Wilcox, W. A. India and Pakistan. (Headline Series no 185) Foreign Policy Association. 345 E. 46th St. New York 10017. '67.
Wilcox, W. A. India, Pakistan, and the rise of China. Walker. '64.
Wiser, C. M. V. and Wiser, W. H. Behind mud walls, 1930-1960. University of California. '63.

PERIODICALS

America. 126:139-42. F. 12, '72. Meaning of Bangladesh. Jerome D'Souza.
American Historical Review. 77:463-72. Ap. '72. Partition of India: a quarter century after. R. E. Frykenberg.
Asian Survey. 9:447-56. Je. '69. Use of the army in nation-building: the case of Pakistan. R. A. Moore, jr.
Asian Survey. 9:614-24. Ag. '69. Russia's role in Indo-Pak politics. S. P. Seth.
Asian Survey. 11:177-84. F. '71. Ceylon: a new government takes office. A. J. Wilson.
Asian Survey. 12:109-15. F. '72. Ceylon: a time of troubles. A. J. Wilson.
Asian Survey. 12:259-74. Mr. '72. April revolt in Ceylon. Politicus, pseud.
Asian Survey. 12:475-92. Je. '72. India: the Soviet stake in stability. R. H. Donaldson.
Asian Survey. 13:187-98. F. '73. Pakistan in 1972: picking up the pieces. Robert La Porte, Jr.
Asian Survey. 13:199-210. F. '73. Bangladesh in 1972: nation-building in a new state. Rounaq Jahan.
Asian Survey. 13:217-30. F. '73. Sri Lanka in 1972: tension and change. W. A. W. Warnapala.
Atlantic. 216:43-8. D. '65. Strong medicine for India. Leland Hazard.
Atlantic. 225:61-3. F. '70. Does foreign aid really aid? The Pearson report. B. D. Nossiter.
Atlantic. 229:18-20+. F. '72. Birth of Bangladesh. F. G. Hutchins.

Bulletin of the Atomic Scientists. 28:4-5. Ap. '72. Bengal: balance of power revisited. Eugene Rabinowitch.

Business Week. p58-9. D. 18, '71. Buoyant economy in a bitter war.

Catholic World. 202:212-16. Ja. '66. Kashmir: a religious war; Muslim and Hindu intolerance. J. F. Drane.

Christian Century. 82:403-4. Mr. 31, '65. Crisis in south India: Hindi made the official language of the Indian union. P. G. Altbach.

Christian Century. 88:806-7. Je. 30, '71. East Pakistan crisis poses grave question for other nations. C. B. Firth.

Christian Century. 89:93-4+. Ja. 26, '72. Bangladesh: the economic outlook. Barbara Howell and Leon Howell.

Christian Century. 89:494-7. Ap. 26, '72. Bangladesh and political parties. Julia Abrahamson.

Commonweal. 98:516-17. S. 28, '73. Shifting mood in India. R. D. N. Dickinson.

Commonwealth. 94:300-1. Je. 11, '71. Insurrection in Ceylon. Tissa Balasuriya.

Contemporary Review. 221:23-8. Jl. '72. East Pakistan 1947-1971. J. E. Owen.

Current History. 52:289-94+. My. '67. Indian-Pakistani relations. R. N. Berkes.

Current History. 54:193-238. Ap. '68. India after Nehru; symposium.

Current History. 63:198-201+. N. '72. Resurgence of India. G. R. Hess.

*Current History. 63:202-5+. N. '72. Pakistan under Bhutto. Khurshid Hyder.

Current History. 63:206-9+. N. '72. Emergence of Bangladesh. J. E. Owen.

Current History. 63:210-13+. N. '72. Sri Lanka today. Urmila Phadnis.

Daedalus. 102:97-113. Winter '73. India and the inner conflict of tradition. J. C. Heesterman.

Department of State Bulletin. 65:721-9. D. 27, '71. U.S. asks UN action to end hostilities in south Asia; statements; with texts of resolution adopted by the Security Council and resolution adopted by the Assembly, December 4-7, 1971. G. H. W. Bush.

Department of State Bulletin. 69:258-9. Ag. 13, '73. U.S. humanitarian assistance to Bangladesh.

*Development Forum. 1:5. Ag.-S. '73. For India: the key to development.

Economist. 236:26+. Jl. 25, '70. Bandaranaike's big battalions.

Economist. 240:28-9. Jl. 31, '71. Time is running out in Bengal.

Economist. 242:31+. F. 26, '72. India spans the old empire like a new colossus.

Economist. 243:38-9. Ap. 1, '72. Bangladesh: between cloud nine and revolution.

Economist. 243:33-4. Je. 24, '72. Sri Lanka: still no money, still no jobs.

Economist. 245:28-9. D. 23, '72. Every region for itself.

Economist. 246:32. Mr. 24, '73. Nowhere to go but up.

Encounter. 37:36-41. O. '71. Anguished thoughts on Bangladesh. Dipak Mazumdar and Peter Wiles.

Far Eastern Economic Review. 76:14-16. Ap. 8, '72. Bangladesh: starting from scratch. S. B. Perera.

Far Eastern Economic Review. 78:26-8. D. 16, '72. Bangladesh: a shaky future; exactly a year after its bloody birth, Asia's newest state is adopting a constitution based on the fundamental principles of nationalism, socialism, democracy and secularism.

Far Eastern Economic Review. 79:23-6. Mr. 12, '73. Politics of division. T. J. S. George.

Far Eastern Economic Review. 80:14+. Ap. 9, '73. Bangladesh: let them eat love. Werner Adam.

Focus. 17:1-6. Ja. '67. Pakistan. A. A. Michel.

Focus. 18:1-8. My. '68. Ceylon. T. R. Joshi.

Focus. 18:8-11. My. '68. Planning for the future. T. R. Joshi.

Forbes. 111:24-5. Mr. 1, '73. Indira Gandhi: interview.

Foreign Affairs. 44:239-52. Ja. '66. Has India an economic future? C. E. Lindblom.

Foreign Affairs. 46:531-47. Ap. '68. Economic development: performance and prospects. M. F. Millikan.

Foreign Affairs. 46:548-61. Ap. '68. Friends and neighbors. W. J. Barnds.

Foreign Affairs. 50:125-35. O. '71. Pakistan divided. S. H. Schanberg.

Foreign Affairs. 50:698-710. Jl. '72. Subcontinent: ménage à trois. Phillips Talbot.

Foreign Affairs. 51:65-77. O. '72. India and the world. Indira (Nehru) Gandhi.

Foreign Affairs. 51:541-54. Ap. '73. Pakistan builds anew. Z. A. Bhutto.

Harper's Magazine. 245:84-92+. Ag. '72. Bangladesh in morning. Laurence Leamer.

Harper's Magazine. 246:26+. Ap. '73. Letter from New Delhi. D. S. Connery.

Holiday. 42:82-3+. N. '67. Vivid variety of India. Laurens van der Post.

Holiday. 42:51-4. D. '67. Letter from Ceylon. Marc Connelly.
Holiday. 47:40-3+. Ap. '70. Ceylon; a larger-than-life travel poster. Gordon Cotler.
Horizon. 7:50-63. Autumn '65. Pearl on the toe of India. Santha Rama Rau.
International Affairs (London). 48:242-9. Ap. '72. Bangladesh: why it happened. G. W. Choudhury.
International Affairs (London). 49:35-50. Ja. '73. Great powers and the Indian sub-continent. Robert Jackson.
International Labour Review. 106:372-7. O. '72. Social policy in Pakistan.
International Labour Review. 107:133-66. F. '73. Tractor mechanization and rural development in Pakistan. C. H. Gotsch.
Journal of Asian Studies. 28:453-68. My. '69. Untouchable soldier: caste, politics and the Indian army. S. P. Cohen.
Journal of International Affairs. 24 no 2:245-71. '70. Implications of a six percent growth rate for Asia. S. H. Wellisz.
Labour Monthly. 54:4-12. Ja. '72. India, Pakistan and Bangladesh.
Life. 58:30-6. Je. 11, '65. War in a windblown waste called the Rann of Kutch.
Life. 71:2-5. D. 31, '71. Anguished birth of Bangladesh.
Mademoiselle. 64:132-4. D. '66. Traveling with *Mademoiselle*: travel, temples and tolerance. Santha Rama Rau.
*Nation. 212:582-4. My. 10, '71. Ceylon: the bitter harvest. Elizabeth Gilliland.
Nation. 213:682-91. D. 27, '71. War nobody stopped. V. G. Kiernan; Rehman Sobhan; V. P. Nanda.
*Nation. 214:134-8. Ja. 31, '72. Future of a subcontinent; Punjab, Bengal & the green revolution. Richard Critchfield.
Nation. 214:297-9. Mr. 6, '72. Bangladesh: fuse in the subcontinent. Paul Deutschman.
Nation. 214:582-4. My. 8, '72. Bangladesh: fertile for mischief. David Loshak.
National Geographic. 129:447-97. Ap. '66. Ceylon. D. K. Grosvenor and G. M. Grosvenor.
National Geographic. 131:1-47. Ja. '67. Problems of a two-part land. Bern Keating.
National Geographic. 142:295-333. S. '72. Bangladesh: hope nourishes a new nation. W. S. Ellis.
National Review. 23:928-9. Ag. 24, '71. Peking's double game. J. M. Van Der Kroef.
National Review. 24:27. Ja. 21, '72. Who will rule Bangladesh. James Burnham.
National Review. 24:240-1. Mr. 3, '72. India. W. F. Buckley, Jr.

New Leader. 56:9-12. Ap. 16, '73. Indira Gandhi's 'peaceful radicalism.' B. P. Menon.

New Republic. 153:6-7. Ag. 7, '65. India's crisis: community development program. Selden Menefee and Audrey Menefee.

New Republic. 154:13-17. Ap. 2, '66. Mrs. Gandhi's mission. Alex Campbell.

New Republic. 157:12. D. 23, '67. India's gigantic effort at modernization. R. L. Strout.

*New Republic. 158:19-21. Je. 22, '68. Indifferent India. B. D. Nossiter.

New Republic. 160:15-19. Mr. 22, '69. Divided they stand. Alex Campbell.

New Republic. 164:9-10. Ap. 17, '71. Bangladesh.

New Republic. 165:7-9. D. 18, '71. India-Pakistan War. A. J. Goldberg.

*New York Times. p 47. Ja. 21, '73. India's planning goes awry. Kasturi Rangan.

New York Times. p E5. Jl. 1, '73. Hunger is the people's enemy. Bernard Weinraub.

New York Times. p 7. Jl. 5, '73. India and Pakistan vying in Mideast. Bernard Weinraub.

*New York Times. p 7. Jl. 14, '73. Karachi, a clean city once, is now a trough of urban squalor. Bernard Weinraub.

*New York Times. p 44. Jl. 17, '73. Pakistan's P.O.W. wives; suffering the stigma of being women alone. Bernard Weinraub.

New York Times. p 2. Jl. 24, '73. Monsoon is the season of death in the slums of Calcutta. Bernard Weinraub.

New York Times. p 2. Jl. 27, '73. Landless untouchables in a poor area start to protest—and die. Bernard Weinraub.

New York Times. p 10. Jl. 29, '73. India is seeking emergency food. Bernard Weinraub.

New York Times. p 1+. Ag. 6, '73. India, in economy drive, cuts birth control efforts. Bernard Weinraub.

New York Times. p 12. Ag. 20, '73. India-Nepal relations running hot and cold. Bernard Weinraub.

New York Times. p 10. O. 5, '73. Bondage of peasants, though illegal, persists in India. Bernard Weinraub.

New York Times. p 8. Ja. 9, '74. Bombay's counterparts of the Black Panthers fume and plot. Bernard Weinraub.

New York Times Magazine. p 27-9+. S. 19, '65. Why Hindu and Moslem speak hate. Kushwant Singh.

New York Times Magazine. p 5+. Ja. 23, '66. We've never had it so bad. Kushwant Singh.

New York Times Magazine. p 29+. Ja. 15, '67. Myths that divide India and us. Lester Markel.

New York Times Magazine. p 58-60+. O. 13, '68. Can India survive Calcutta? Joseph Lelyveld.

New York Times Magazine. p 26-7+. F. 15, '70. Indian expatriate rediscovers India. Dom Moraes.

New York Times Magazine. p 26-7+. Ja. 10, '71. East Pakistan: the wave. D. F. Moraes.

New York Times Magazine. p 11-13+. Ja. 9, '72. Lament for Pakistan; failure of the impossible dream. J. A. Michener.

New York Times Magazine. p 9+. Ja. 30, '72. Homecoming in Bangladesh. Kushwant Singh.

New York Times Magazine. p 7+. Je. 25, '72. Bhutto picks up the pieces of Pakistan. J. P. Sterba.

New York Times Magazine. p 46-7+. N. 19, '72. Peace may finally come to Shangri-La. Aubrey Menen.

New York Times Magazine. p 8-9+. D. 31, '72. Indira Gandhi is sort of the de Gaulle of India. Aubrey Menen.

New York Times Magazine. p 14-15+. Ja. 21, '73. Bangladesh, after the first year: will it ever be a workable country? Kushwant Singh.

New York Times Magazine. p 30-2+. Ag. 26, '73. Waiting for the monsoon. Kushwant Singh.

New Yorker. 46:97-8+. Mr. 21, '70. Profiles; missionaries of charity, Calcutta. Ved Mehta.

New Yorker. 47:166+. D. 11, '71. Letter from West Bengal. Ved Mehta.

New Yorker. 47:40-2+. F. 12; 89-96+. F. 19, '72. Reporter at large. Robert Shaplen.

Newsweek. 73:38-9. Ap. 7, '69. Pakistan: why Ayub quit.

Newsweek. 74:55-7. D. 15, '69. Report from Mrs. Gandhi's India. Edward Behr.

Newsweek. 76:34-6. N. 30, '70. Pakistan tragedy: cyclone; with report and interviews. Maynard Parker.

Newsweek. 78:26-30. Ag. 2, '71. Bengal: the murder of a people; with reports by Loren Jenkins and Tony Clifton.

Newsweek. 78:50+. N. 15, '71. Unwinnable war. Arnaud de Borchgrave.

Newsweek. 79:20-1. Ja. 3, '72. Birth pangs of Bangladesh.

*Newsweek. 79:35-9. Mr. 27, '72. Bangladesh: the fight for survival.

Newsweek. 79:33-4+. Ap. 10, '72. Perils of Pakistan.

Newsweek. 80:23. Jl. 3, '72. In search of a durable peace.

Newsweek. 80:60+. D. 11, '72. One year after. Loren Jenkins.

Newsweek. 82:43. Jl. 16, '73. Life with Bhutto. Loren Jenkins.

Orbis. 16:952-74. Winter '73. Pakistan's security problem: a bill of constraints. A. H. Syed.

Pacific Affairs. 44:511-26. Winter '71-'72. Political re-alignment in India. Pran Chopra.

Pacific Affairs. 45:75-91. Spring '72. Economic development in China and India: some conditioning factors. Barry Richman.

Pacific Affairs. 45:191-205. Summer '72. Bangladesh & after. M. S. Rajan.

Pacific Affairs. 45:372-86. Fall '72. In the wake of Bangladesh: a new role for India in Asia? S. J. Heginbotham.

Pacific Affairs. 45:556-72. Winter '72-'73. Pakistani nationalism reconsidered. S. M. M. Qureshi.

Pacific Affairs. 45:573-81. Winter '72-'73. Pakistan and the consequences of Bangladesh; review article. E. L. Tepper.

Pacific Affairs. 46:59-76. Spring '73. Constitution-making in Bangladesh. A. F. Huq.

Political Science Quarterly. 88:86-93. Mr. '73. Revolution and growth: two case studies from India. T. A. Timberg.

Ramparts Magazine. 10:26-9. Jl. '71. Civil war in Ceylon. Tamara Deutscher.

Reader's Digest. 87:167-8+. Ag. '65. Families are different in India. Santha Rama Rau.

Reader's Digest. 98:90-4. My. '71. Terrible wave: Ganges Delta disaster. J. P. Blank.

Reader's Digest. 99:66-71. N. '71. Agony of East Pakistan. David Reed and J. E. Frazer.

Reporter. 35:36-8. Ag. 11, '66. Paradise island, entire unto itself. F. V. Grunfeld.

Reporter. 36:40-2. Ja. 12, '67. Pakistan feels the pains of division; autonomy movement in East Pakistan. M. H. Zim.

Round Table. 59:302-7. Jl. '69. East Pakistan's revolt against Ayub. Rehman Sobhan.

*Saturday Review. 52:12-16. Ag. 9, '69. Can India make it? R. R. R. Brooks.

Saturday Review. 53:24+. D. 12, '70. East Pakistan and the U.S. Norman Cousins.
    Reply with rejoinder. 54:22 Ja. 9, '71. R. D. Murphy.

Saturday Review. 54:32-3+. N. 6, '71. Bangladesh: on the brink of survival. C. S. Baldwin.

Saturday Review. 55:23-7. F. 5, '72. Pakistan's costly delusion. Rosanne Klass.

Senior Scholastic. 93:20-1. N. 8, '68. Two wings; separate but united.

Senior Scholastic. 99:14-15. Ja. 10, '72. India vs. Pakistan: the war nobody wanted; questions and answers.

Senior Scholastic. 100:4-8+. Mr. 6, '72. Bangladesh: picking up the pieces.

Sunset. 143:41-2+. N. '69. In India, a visitor is caught up in history.

Sunset. 144:58+. F. '70. Game preserves, beach resorts, temples, jungle: Ceylon is a discovery.

Time. 90:26+. Ag. 25, '67. Two decades of independence.

Time. 93:26+. F. 21, '69. Fires of hatred.

Time. 95:41-2. My. 25, '70. Fire and blood again.

Time. 95:35-6. Je. 8, '70. Dry eyed and flying high.

Time. 96:28+. D. 7, '70. East Pakistan: the politics of catastrophe.

Time. 99:30. F. 28, '72. Bleak future. D.Coggin.

Time. 100:21-2. Ag. 21, '72. Austere 25th birthday.

Time. 101:38-9. F. 5, '73. Jai Andhra! statehood movement of Andhra Pradesh.

Time. 101:24+. Mr. 5, '73. Under the velvet glove.

Time. 101:50+. My. 21, '73. Forgotten hostages of peace.

Time. 102:40+. S. 17, '73. Wrapping up the war; agreement reached on prisoners.

Travel. 126:56-62. O. '66. Wonders of India. J. P. Gabriel.

Travel. 128:30-5+. S. '67. Ceylon sidetrip. E. S. Smith.

Travel. 136:28-35+. S. '71. Instant India. R. H. Peck.

Travel & Camera. 33:34-6+. N. '70. Serene satisfactions of a visit to Ceylon. Bernard Taper.

UN Monthly Chronicle. 10:34-6. F. '73. Relief operation in Bangladesh.

UNESCO Courier. 26:53-5. Ag.-S. '73. Life-saving 'killas' of Bangladesh.

U.S. News & World Report. 61:68-71. N. 28, '66. India: a huge country on the verge of collapse. S. W. Saunders.

U.S. News & World Report. 62:90-3. Ap. 3, '67. Too many people; is India facing disaster? interview. S. Chandrasekhar.

U.S. News & World Report. 63:74-6. S. 4, '67. New hope for India, but: still a nation on the brink.

U.S. News & World Report. 66:77-80. F. 17, '69. India: a giant country deep in trouble. J. N. Wallace.

U.S. News & World Report. 68:63-4. My. 25, '70. Good news from Asia: India is beginning to move.

*U.S. News & World Report. 71:86-9. N. 8, '71. India's endless troubles, and why they worry U.S.

U.S. News & World Report. 71:21-2. D. 6, '71. Why India and Pakistan are at it again.

U.S. News & World Report. 71:12-13. D. 20, '71. Hindus vs. Moslems: conflict that goes back 450 years.

U.S. News & World Report. 71:20-3. D. 27, '71. In wake of India's victory, storm signals still flying [political and economic conditions in Bangladesh and West Pakistan]. J. N. Wallace.

U.S. News & World Report. 72:79. Ja. 17, '72. Can one man save a stricken nation? J. N. Wallace.

U.S. News & World Report. 72:74-6. F. 28, '72. Price India must pay for its two-week war.

U.S. News & World Report. 72:72-5. Ap. 3, '72. From revolution to reality: birth pangs of a nation; report from Bangladesh. J. N. Wallace.

U.S. News & World Report. 73:35. S. 18, '72. Playing politics with 93,000 Pakistani captives.

Vital Speeches of the Day. 35:200-2. Ja. 15, '69. Developing society; address, December 1, 1968. Mohammad Ayub Khan.

Vital Speeches of the Day. 39:476-8. My. 15, '73. Future of democracy in India; address, March 26, 1973. J. C. English.

Wall Street Journal. p 1+. N. 9, '71. New worry in Asia: Washington's relations with India deteriorate as Moscow's improve; apparent American support of Pakistan angers Delhi to benefit of the Soviets. P. R. Kann.

Wall Street Journal. p 1+. N. 26, '71. Rhetoric & reality: India, Pakistan fight war of words—& guns. P. R. Kann.

*Wall Street Journal. p 1+. Jc. 6, '73. Parched land: in India, many are hungry; more will be unless the rains come. W. D. Hartley.

War on Hunger. 6:8-11+. D. '72. 'But what of Pakistan?' Sidney Sober.

*Washington Post. p 1+. D. 18, '72. On 1st anniversary, Bangladesh's future still a question mark. L. M. Simons.

World Politics. 21:448-68. Ap. '69. Democracy and political development; perspectives from the Indian experience. [review article] F. R. Frankel.

World Today. 25:36-46. Ja. '69. China as a factor in Indo-Pakistani politics. S. P. Seth.

World Today. 27:372-9. S. '71. East Bengal: a crisis for India. Pran Chopra.

Yale Review. 55:552-69. Je. '66. Pakistan's search for national identity. D. D. Anderson.